The Screens

OTHER WORKS BY JEAN GENET
published by Grove Press

The Balcony
The Blacks: A Clown Show
Funeral Rites
The Maids and Deathwatch
Miracle of The Rose
Our Lady of the Flowers
Querelle
The Thief's Journal

The Screens

A PLAY IN SEVENTEEN SCENES BY
JEAN GENET

Translated from the French by
Bernard Frechtman

GROVE PRESS □ NEW YORK

Originally published as *Les Paravents* by Marc Barbezat, Décines, Isère, France, 1961

Published by Grove Press, Inc.
920 Broadway
New York, N.Y. 10010

The Library of Congress has cataloged the first printing of this title as follows:

Genêt, Jean, 1910-
      The screens; a play in seventeen scenes. Translated from the French by Bernard Frechtman. New York, Grove Press [1962]

     201 p.

     I. Title.

PQ2613.E53P33   1962   842.912   62-13055 ‡

Manufactured in the United States of America
10 9 8 7 6 5 4 3 2 1

To the memory of one who died young

THE CHARACTERS

(in order of appearance)

Saïd	Madani
The Mother	The Gendarme
Mustapha	Mr. Blankensee
Warda	Malik
Brahim	Abdil
Malika	Nasser
The Maid	The Lieutenant
Ahmed	Preston
Leila	The Sergeant
Sir Harold	Voice of Walter
Habib	Voice of Hernandez
Taleb	Voice of Brandineschi
Chigha	The Guard
Kadidja	The Voice
Nedjma	Mrs. Blankensee
Habiba	The Dignitary
The Woman	The Chief
The Flute Player	The Academician
The Policeman	The Soldier
The Cadi	The Vamp
The Man Who Pissed	The Photographer
The Second Policeman	The Judge

The Banker	Felton
The General	Srir
The Little Girl	Bachir
The Man	The Soldier
The Woman	Hamed
The Arab	Salem
Kaddur	Ommu
The Son	Djemila
M'Barek	Si Slimane
Lahussein	Nestor
M'Hamed	Roger
Larbi	Jojo
Ali	Roland
Kuider	Riton
Amer	The Arabs
Attrache	Aicha
Azuz	Aziza
Abdesselem	Hossein
Monsieur Bonneuil	Smaïl
Madame Bonneuil	The Grocer
Lalla	The Clerk
Srira	The Legionnaire
The Arab Woman	The Missionary
The Gendarme's Wife	The Husband
Morales	The Combatant
Helmut	The Second Combatant
Pierre	The Third Combatant

Each actor will be required to play five or six roles, male or
female.

SOME DIRECTIONS

This is how the play should be staged:

In an open-air theater. A rectangular area enclosed within a very high, board fence. For the audience: tiers of any material one wishes. The back and sides of the stage are to be formed by high, uneven boards, painted black. They are to be arranged in such a way that platforms of different heights can be brought onstage from the left and right. There will thus be an extremely varied set of stages, levels, and surfaces. The screens and actors will enter and leave through spaces between the boards, right and left.

One or more real objects must always be on the stage, in contrast with the objects drawn in *trompe-l'oeil* on each screen. The objects are to be brought in as follows: when the audience enters, a milestone and a rock pile are already onstage. When the audience has been seated, a screen, moved by a man behind it, arrives from the right wing. This screen slides in such a way that it is set up behind the milestone and the rock pile.

THE SET:

It will be formed by a series of screens, each about ten feet high, on which objects and landscapes will be painted.

They are to be moved in absolute silence. They should there-fore be mounted on tiny rubber-lined wheels which, in addition, roll on a stage carpet. Behind the screen is a stagehand whose job is to move it.

There is to be a short period of darkness between scenes for the change of set.

Near the screen there must always be at least one real object (wheelbarrow, bucket, bicycle, etc.), the function of which is to establish a contrast between its own reality and the objects that are drawn.

THE CHARACTERS:

If possible, they will be masked. If not, highly made-up, painted (even the soldiers). Excessive make-up, contrasting with the realism of the costumes. It is best to provide a large variety of false noses—I shall indicate the form of some of these as the characters appear. At times, false chins as well. All this should be artfully harmonized with the colors of the costumes. No face should retain the conventional beauty of feature which is played up all too often on both stage and screen. In addition to the imagination of directors, there are thousands of new plastics that can be used in presenting plays nowadays.

The Arabs are to wear very curly, oakum wigs. Their complexion is—as the expression goes—swarthy.

THE ACTING:

To be extremely precise. Very taut. No useless gestures. Every gesture must be *visible*.

SCENE ONE

Four-paneled screen. Painted on the screen: a palm tree, an Arab grave.

At the foot of the screen, a rock pile. Left, a milestone on which is written: AÏN/SOFAR, 2 Miles.
Blue light, very harsh.

SAÏD's *costume: green trousers, red jacket, tan shoes, white shirt, mauve tie, pink cap.*
THE MOTHER's *costume: violet satin dress, patched all over in different shades of violet. Big yellow veil. She is barefooted. Each of her toes is painted a different—and violent—color.*

SAÏD *(twenty years old), tie askew. His jacket is completely buttoned. He enters from behind the screen. As soon as he is visible to the audience, he stops, as if exhausted. He turns toward the wing from which he entered and cries out.*

SAÏD: Rose! (*A pause.*) I said rose! The sky's already pink as a rose. The sun'll be up in half an hour. . . . (*He waits, rests on one foot, and wipes his face.*) Don't you want me to help you? (*Silence.*) Why? No one can see us. (*He wipes his shoes with his handkerchief. He straightens up.*) Watch out! (*He is about to rush forward, but remains stock-still, watchful.*) No, no, it was a grass snake. (*He speaks less loudly as the invisible person seems to draw closer. His tone finally becomes normal.*) I told you to put your shoes on.

Enter an old Arab woman, all wrinkled. Violet dress, yellow veil. Barefooted. On her head, a cardboard valise. She too has emerged from behind the screen, but from the other side. She is holding her shoes—a red button-boot and a white pump.

THE MOTHER: I want them to be clean when I get there.

SAÏD (*crossly*): You think *they'll* have clean shoes? And new shoes besides? And even clean feet?

THE MOTHER (*now coming up to* SAÏD): What do you expect? That they have new feet?

SAÏD: Don't joke. Today I want to stay sad. I'd hurt myself on purpose to be sad. There's a rock pile. Go take a rest.

He takes the valise, which she is carrying on her head, and puts it down at the foot of the palm tree. THE MOTHER *sits down.*

THE MOTHER (*smiling*): Sit down.

SAÏD: No. The stones are too soft for my ass. I want everything to make me feel blue.

THE MOTHER (*still smiling*): You want to stay sad? I find your situation comical. You, my only son, are marrying the ugliest woman in the next town and all the towns around, and your mother has to walk six miles to go celebrate your marriage. (*She kicks the valise.*) And to bring the family a valise full of presents. (*Laughing, she kicks again and the valise falls.*)

SAÏD (*sadly*): You'll break everything if you keep it up.

THE MOTHER (*laughing*): So what? Wouldn't you get a kick out of opening, in front of her eyes, a valise full of bits of porcelain, crystal, lace, bits of mirror, salami. . . . Anger may make her beautiful.

SAÏD: Her resentment will make her funnier looking.

THE MOTHER *(still laughing)*: If you laugh until you cry, your tears'll bring her face into focus. But the point is, you wouldn't have the courage . . .

SAÏD: To . . .

THE MOTHER *(still laughing)*: To treat her as an ugly woman. You're going to her reluctantly. Vomit on her.

SAÏD *(gravely)*: Should I really? What's she done to marry me? Nothing.

THE MOTHER: As much as you have. She's left over because she's ugly. And you, because you're poor. She needs a husband, you a wife. She and you take what's left, you take each other. *(She laughs. She looks at the sky.)* Yes, sir, it'll be hot. God's bringing us a day of light.

SAÏD *(after a silence)*: Don't you want me to carry the valise? No one would see you. I'll give it back to you when we get to town.

THE MOTHER: God and you would see me. With a valise on your head you'd be less of a man.

SAÏD *(very surprised)*: Does a valise on your head make you more of a woman?

THE MOTHER: God and you . . .

SAÏD: God? With a valise on my head? I'll carry it in my hand. *(She says nothing. After a silence, pointing to the valise)*: What did you pay for the piece of yellow velvet?

THE MOTHER: I didn't pay for it. I did laundry at the home of the Jewess.

SAÏD *(counting in his head)*: Laundry? What do you get for each job?

THE MOTHER: She doesn't usually pay me. She lends me her donkey every Friday. And what did the clock cost you? It doesn't run, true enough, but it's a clock. . . .

SAÏD: It's not paid for yet. . . . I still have sixty feet of wall to mason. Djellul's barn. I'll do it the day after tomorrow. What about the coffee grinder?

THE MOTHER: And the eau de Cologne?

SAÏD: Didn't cost much. But I had to go to Aïn Targ to get it. Eight miles there, eight miles back.

THE MOTHER (*smiling*): Perfumes for your princess! (*Suddenly, she listens.*) What's that?

SAÏD (*looking into the distance, left*): Monsieur Leroy and his wife on the national highway.

THE MOTHER: If we'd stopped at the crossing, they might have given us a lift.

SAÏD: Us?

THE MOTHER: Normally they wouldn't have, but you'd have explained that it's your wedding day . . . that you're in a hurry to see the bride . . . and I'd have so enjoyed seeing myself arrive in a car.

A silence.

SAÏD: Want to eat something? There's the roast chicken in a corner of the valise.

THE MOTHER (*gravely*): You're crazy, it's for the meal. If a leg were missing, they'd think I raised crippled chickens. We're poor, she's ugly, but not enough to deserve one-legged chickens.

A silence.

SAÏD: Won't you put your shoes on? I've never seen you in high-heeled shoes.

THE MOTHER: I've worn them twice in my life. The first time, the day of your father's funeral. Suddenly I was up so high I saw myself on a tower looking down at my grief that remained on the ground, where they were burying your

father. One of the shoes, the left one, I found in a garbage
can. The other, by the wash-house. The second time
I wore them was when I had to receive the bailiff who
wanted to foreclose on the shanty. (*She laughs.*) A dry
board shanty, dry but rotten, rotten but resonant, so
resonant you could see our noises zooming by, only them,
our noises shooting through, your father's and mine, our
noises reflected by a slope, we lived there, slept there, in
that drum, as in broad daylight, which let our life shoot
through the rotten boards where our sounds, our noises,
our voices shot through, a rip-roaring place that shanty!
And the bailiff wanting to foreclose on it, but me . . .
standing there, on the tips of my toes and resting on my
heels, I felt mighty proud, and even haughty. My head was
touching the corrugated tin. I pointed to the door and
put the bailiff out.

SAÏD: Good for you, mother! Put on your high-heeled shoes.

THE MOTHER: But child, there's still two miles to go. My feet'll
hurt and I may break the heels.

SAÏD (*very sternly*): Put on your shoes. (*He hands her the shoes, one
white, the other red.* THE MOTHER *puts them on without a word.
He looks at her while she straightens up.*) You're beautiful in
them. Keep them on, and dance! Dance! (*She takes two
or three steps, like a model, quite elegantly in fact.*) Keep
dancing, madame. And you, palm trees, lift your hair,
lower your heads—or brows, as they say—so you can look
at my old lady. And, for a second, let the wind stop short,
let it look, *there's* the party! (*To* THE MOTHER): Dance,
old girl, on your unbreakable legs, dance! (*He bends down
and speaks to the stones.*) And you too, pebbles, look at
what's going on above you. Let my old lady stamp on
you like a revolution on the king's highway. . . . Hurrah!
. . . Boom! Boom! (*He imitates a cannon.*) Boom! Zoom!
Boom! (*He roars with laughter.*)

THE MOTHER (*echoing him, while dancing*): And boom! . . . And
bang! . . . Whang! Zoom! Boom! . . . boom! . . . On
the king's highway. (*To* SAÏD): Go on, imitate lightning!
SAÏD (*still laughing*): .And boom! And whang! Whee! . . .
Whaaw! . . . Zeee! (*He imitates lightning with his voice and
gestures.*)
THE MOTHER (*still dancing*): Whang! . . . Boom! . . . Whaaw
. . . Zeee! (*She imitates lightning.*)
SAÏD: Boom! . . . Boom! My dancing mother, my prancing
mother is streaming with sweat. (*He looks at her from a
distance.*) Streams of it rolling down from your temples to
your cheeks, from your cheeks to your tits, from your
tits to your belly. . . . And you, dust, take a look at
my mother, see how beautiful and proud she is beneath
the sweat and on her high heels! (THE MOTHER *keeps
smiling and dancing.*) You're beautiful. I'll carry the valise.
Whee! . . .

He imitates lightning. He reaches for the valise, but THE MOTHER
*grabs it first. A brief struggle. They burst out laughing, imitate
thunder and lightning. The valise falls to the ground and opens, and
everything falls out: it was empty.* SAÏD *and* THE MOTHER *fall to the
ground and sit there roaring with laughter.*

THE MOTHER (*laughing and holding out her hands to catch invisible
drops*): It's a storm. The whole wedding'll be drenched.

They leave, shivering, that is, they go behind the screen.

SCENE TWO

The brothel. Two screens. Seated at a table covered with a multi-colored cloth, right, are three clients. The two whores are standing motionless, left.

Costumes of the two whores:
MALIKA: *Gold lamé dress, high-heeled black shoes, a kind of gilt, oriental tiara. Her hair falls on her shoulders. She is twenty years old.*
WARDA: *Dress of very heavy gold lamé, high-heeled red shoes, her hair coiled up in a huge blood-red chignon. Her face is very pale. She is about forty.*

The men sitting in the brothel are wearing shabby, Italian-style suits (short jacket, narrow trousers) of different shades of gray. Each is wearing a shirt of violent color: red, green, yellow, blue.

WARDA *has a very long and very thin false nose.*

A MAID *is kneeling at* WARDA'*s feet and applying grease paint to them.* WARDA *is wearing a pink petticoat as full as a crinoline. Nearby, on a wicker dummy, a gold petticoat and cloak.*

MUSTAPHA (*making an observation*): You're the more beautiful.

WARDA (*to* THE MAID, *in a drawling voice*): Thick . . . thicker, the white on my ankles . . . (*She is picking her teeth with a kind of long gilt-headed hatpin.*) It's the white that keeps the skin taut. . . . (*She spits out, far off, what she had between her teeth.*) Completely decayed . . . The whole back of my mouth is in ruins.

MUSTAPHA (*to* BRAHIM, *in a very sharp tone*): A whore's job is harder than ours.

The three men keep watching the preparations, open-mouthed.

WARDA (*counting her bracelets*): There's one missing. You'll bring it in. I have to be heavy. (*A pause, and then, as if to herself.*) A bracelet missing! As if I were a coffin and a hammerstroke were missing. (*To* MUSTAPHA): The night begins with dressing up, with painting. When the sun's gone down, I can't do a thing without my finery . . . not even spread my legs to piss, but rigged up in gold I'm the Queen of Showers.

THE MAID *stands up and hands her the gold petticoat. Then, the ringing of a bell, indicating that a door is closing. From behind the screen, left, emerges a soldier of the Foreign Legion. He finishes buckling his belt and leaves, that is, he goes behind the second screen. Then* MALIKA *appears. A little less hieratic than* WARDA, *but nevertheless haughty and sulky. Pale face, with green make-up. She stops when she reaches* WARDA, *but without looking at anyone.*

WARDA (*to* THE MAID): Now the hands. First the grease paint. And on the white you draw the veins. Blue. (THE MAID, *who has a number of little paint pots, starts painting* WARDA's *hands. To* MALIKA): He wanted you to . . .?

MALIKA (*motionless*): Dane or no Dane. I'm not a waitress.

WARDA:. . . . to get undressed? (MALIKA *does not reply, but* BRAHIM *and* MUSTAPHA *burst out laughing.*) You were right to refuse. Fix your belt.

MALIKA *winds herself in a very long, gold muslin belt which was coming undone.*

BRAHIM (*standing up; in a very clear, very precise voice*): In France, when you go to a whorehouse, the whore undresses. I'm talking about smart joints, those with chandeliers on the ceiling and an assistant madame in a hat with feathers. In a hat with flowers and feathers. (*A pause.*) And a chin strap under her chin.

WARDA (*severely and wearily*): Do you know what there is in the hem of my skirt? (*To* THE MAID): You'll pick a rose.

THE MAID: A celluloid one?

BRAHIM (*laughing, to* WARDA): It's heavy, in any case.

WARDA (*to* THE MAID): Red velvet. (*To* BRAHIM): Lead. Lead in the hems of my three petticoats. (*The two men burst out laughing.* MALIKA, *still solemn, takes two or three steps.*) It takes a man's hand to turn them up, a man's hand or mine.

The men laugh. MALIKA *takes a hatpin from her hair and picks her teeth.*

MALIKA: Not just anyone can approach our thighs. One must knock before entering.

WARDA (*haughtily, same drawling, disillusioned voice*): Twenty-four years! A whore's not something you can improvise. She has to ripen. It took me twenty-four years. And I'm gifted! A man, what's that? A man remains a man. In our presence, it's he who strips like a whore from Cherbourg or Le Havre. (*To* THE MAID): The red velvet rose. But dust it.

THE MAID *leaves*.

MUSTAPHA (*standing up*): The French were pretty annoyed about our fucking their whores.

WARDA (*with exaggerated contempt*): Did they let you do anything else? They didn't. So? Here what do you fuck? Us. The beauties weighted with leaded petticoats, when you've scraped together enough money in the sun, in the vineyards, or at night, in the mines, to pay us. It's because we carry the treasures of the vines and mines under our skirts.

MUSTAPHA (*to* BRAHIM): She doesn't think we'd have the courage . . .

MALIKA (*interrupting him*): Courage on a bicycle. When you pedal fast so as to make smutty remarks to the postmistress as you go by. Si Slimane . . .

BRAHIM (*interrupting* MALIKA): Him again!

WARDA: Because there's no one like him. (*A pause.*) Unfortunately for us.

MALIKA: On his horse, in sixteen villages at the same time. A Kabyl from Saada told me that he had appeared on his horse in sixteen villages at the same time, but that in actual fact he was resting in the shade, at the side of a road. . . .

BRAHIM (*laughing*): At the side of a road, of a pink lip or of two brown lips? And standing on sixteen horses?

MALIKA: To our misfortune. I was told so by a miner from Taroudent who was on his way home from work at two in the afternoon, because he'd injured himself. . . .

WARDA (*irritated, and in a sharper tone*): What she says about it is for the joy of the words, the delight of conversation, because if we had the misfortune to take the country's misfortunes seriously, then farewell our misfortune and farewell our pleasures.

BRAHIM (*to* MALIKA): What was he injured with, the miner?

MALIKA: . . . his injury. Told me so. A butcher from the medina told me so. The Sidi Hamed postman told me so. A midwife her man told me so, my belt's unbuckling.

WARDA (*very annoyed, yet admiringly*): Again! Let me have it. (*She takes the red velvet rose which* THE MAID, *who has just entered, hands her. She shakes it and blows on it.*)

MUSTAPHA (*to* MALIKA): They tell *you* everything.

MALIKA: A man comes for me, my belt unbuckles. This is the brothel, the men empty themselves, they tell me everything.

BRAHIM (*with a burst of laughter*): When your belt flies open . . .

MALIKA (*gravely*): . . . it's spreading its sails, a man's on the way, bringing me cash. My dresses, my pins, my laces, my snap-buttons know it before I do. They sniff the hot meat. If a man, or a mail clerk, a kid, a policeman or an old geezer merely thinks of me, approaches or only looks in the direction of the neighborhood, my belt and dress scoot off. If I didn't hold them back with both hands . . .

They all burst out laughing, except WARDA.

WARDA (*to* THE MAID, *drawling, as before*): Remember to empty the basin. (*To* MALIKA): And when a man's meat calls *me* to the rescue, dresses, petticoats, jackets pile up on my shoulders and buttocks. They come out of the trunks, standing up, to array me. You knock yourself out, Malika. A real whore should be able to attract by what she's reduced herself to being. I worked for years at my tooth cleaning with a hatpin. My style! (*The two men, who are standing, approach her with very tiny steps and stare at her.*) Not too close. (*She makes a gesture at them with her hatpin to make them keep their distance. The men stop short and stare at her. A silence.*)

WARDA (*to* THE MAID, *after picking her teeth*): Put some more grease on my hair. (*A pause, then, to* MUSTAPHA): You're right not to believe in the hope that gallops on sixteen horses at the same time, but . . .

MUSTAPHA (*gravely*): In order to see you I come from the phosphate mines. I see you, it's you I believe in, the more you clothe, the more you plaster yourself . . .

WARDA: My outfits! Underneath, there's not much left . . .

MUSTAPHA (*coming a step closer*): What if death were there . . .

WARDA (*stopping him with a gesture*): It's there. Quietly at work. You were talking about horses. . . .

AHMED (*springing to his feet*): Is hatred of the foreigners there?

MALIKA (*surprised, but staring at* AHMED): Under my belt? The fire that burns you there when you enter comes from that.

AHMED: Is it there?

BRAHIM (*placing his hand on his heart, but still staring at* WARDA): A hundred years after my death it will still be there.

AHMED: Is it there?

MUSTAPHA (*still staring at* WARDA): . . . in my underpants? It strikes harder there than in Brahim's heart. It burns hotter there than under Malika's belt.

AHMED: Is it . . .

WARDA (*curtly, her voice suddenly very firm*): Crap. The earth—though the darkness surrounding the whorehouse is thick —the earth of the walls is porous. And your wives listen in, the way one listens to the radio. (*She spits out what she has just extracted from a tooth.*)

AHMED: If it's under your belts and behind our flies, why shouldn't hope come running by there?

MALIKA: Because it wouldn't gallop on sixteen horses, amidst sixteen paths, to rest there in the shade . . . (*To* AHMED, *provocatively*): If you come up with me, if you feel like it, I'll let you have it at cost.

WARDA (*curtly*): Crap. (*She bursts into very strident, very long*

laughter. A silence. A kind of anger suddenly comes over her.)
Odd words now, plucked from the pages of newspapers
and booklets. That's what comes from being in a whorehouse and not wanting to be a total whore, down to the
skeleton. (*To* THE MAID): My cloak.

THE MAID *goes to get the cloak, which is on the wicker dummy, and*
returns with it while WARDA *breaks out again into the same laughter.*

AHMED (*still in a state of excitement*): What if . . .

Ringing of the bell of an entrance door which is opened and then closed.
They all stop talking and look. WARDA *turns around and makes*
a gesture. Then they all—except the two women—restrain a desire to
laugh.

WARDA (*speaking into the wing, and pushing back* MUSTAPHA *who*
  was approaching): Unbutton yourself, Saïd, I'm coming up.
  (*To* THE MAID): The basin?

THE MAID: Rinsed.

WARDA *goes behind a screen, very solemnly. A rather long silence.*

MALIKA: He has to go first, he's had her booked since the eve
  of his wedding.

THE MAID, *who has knelt at her feet, starts polishing her nails. The*
men and then THE MAID *step back into the right wing, while* MALIKA
goes straight ahead into the same wing.

SCENE THREE

A four-paneled screen, which cuts the right corner of the stage, represents the interior of SAÏD's *house. A very poor interior. On the screen are drawn an oven, four pots, a frying pan, and a table. Near the screen are a bucket and a very low stool.*

LEILA's *face will always be covered with a kind of black hood in which three holes have been pierced, two for the eyes and one for the mouth.*

THE MOTHER *is wearing her violet satin dress. She will wear it eternally.*

When the light goes on, LEILA *is alone. She is running and skipping around a pair of worn, patched trousers (with multicolored patches) which is standing upright toward the left side of the stage.*

LEILA *beckons to the trousers to approach. They do not move. Bending forward, she therefore goes to them with tiny steps. She plants herself in front of them. She speaks to them:*

LEILA: Well, won't you move? You go strolling about at night in my dreams, you let the wind blow up your legs, but in my presence you play dead. And yet you're alive, warm, ready for anything, for walking, pissing, spitting, coughing, smoking, farting like a man, and mounting a horse, and being mounted by me. . . .

We hear, off-stage, the cooing of pigeons, the clucking of hens, the crowing of a cock, the bark of a dog. All this is very sonorous and as if slightly parodic.

. . . no doubt about it, you're better built than Saïd. Even though your thighs are shaped like his, yours are more shapely. (*She walks about the trousers and looks at them very attentively.*) Your behind is rounder than his. (*A pause.*) But you don't piss as far. Come, jump on me. If only you could manage to walk three yards—from here to the door —after that, it would be easy, we'd disappear, you and I, in the bushes . . . under the plum tree . . . behind the wall . . . behind another wall . . . the mountain, the sea . . . and me on your rump, on the rounded saddle of your two buttocks, I'd give you a run for your money. . . . (*In front of the trousers, she imitates a horsewoman.*) Giddy-ap! Come on! Giddy-ap! Giddy-ap! I'm whipping you, driving you, wearing you out, and when we get to the foot of the wall, I'll unbutton you, rebutton you, and with my hands in the pockets . . .

THE MOTHER (*behind the screen*): Don't come in. You've had your grain for the day.

We hear the same barnyard cries: chickens, cocks, dog, pig. LEILA *takes the trousers, sits on the floor and starts to sew.*

THE MOTHER (*enters; it is she who has been imitating the animals. She continues for a moment, then*): To a pair of pants! Declarations of love to a pair of patched pants. And thinking it would give you a ride! (*She shrugs.*) It's better

I tell you once and for all, and in plain language, because he won't dare. And he's not good-natured, like me: you're hideous.

LEILA (*continuing to sew*): When I was beautiful . . .

THE MOTHER: Hideous. Don't slobber on your hood.

LEILA: . . . beautiful . . . at night . . .

THE MOTHER: You're kept under glass, like Roquefort cheese, because of the flies.

LEILA: At night, you think I marry Saïd who hasn't a penny? And who's not good-looking? And whom no woman ever looks at? What woman has ever turned around to look at Saïd?

THE MOTHER (*points to a spot on the trousers*): And your patch that's inside out, it turned around to look at what?

LEILA (*looking at the trousers*): So it is. Why, so it is! It put itself on inside out. Saïd'll be heartbroken.

THE MOTHER: He couldn't care less. He knows what pants are. He puts his big legs into them, his ass and all the rest. His rank and titles. If he lays out his pants for the night, it's they who keep watch on a chair, it's they who guard you and frighten you. They keep watch, they keep their eye on you. Saïd can doze away. He knows that pants have to live, and it's the patches that keep them on their toes, and the liveliest are those that are inside out. Don't worry. Saïd's like me, he doesn't mind things being loused up and tearing off in all directions till they reach some star or other, till the moment when trouble—are you listening to me?—grows so great that your husband'll burst. With laughter. Will burst. With laughter. Since you're ugly, be idiotic. And don't slobber.

LEILA: If I slobber more, that's proof I'm becoming more idiotic.

A gigantic shadow—that of SAÏD—*appears on the white wall which forms the background of the stage. It remains motionless. The two women do not see it.*

THE MOTHER: When night comes, you'll go to the wash house. You'll do the washing by moonlight. That'll chap the skin of your fingers a little.

LEILA: And the clucking of the chickens, you think . . .

THE MOTHER: The farm's useful. I want a barnyard around us. And I want it to come out of our bellies. Can you do the rooster?

LEILA (*intently*): Cock . . . cock . . . cock-a-doodle-doo!

THE MOTHER (*angrily*): That's a damaged rooster. I won't have it! Do it again.

LEILA (*in a vibrant voice*): Cock-a-doodle-dooo!

We hear a clearing of the throat, as if someone were going to spit. SAÏD has drawn closer. He is now visible. He is carrying a knapsack on his shoulder. Without looking at anyone, he stops and throws it down. Then he spits.

SAÏD: The cheese was mixed with the jam. I ate my bread dry. (*To* LEILA, *who was about to get up*): Remain squatting. Keep sewing.

THE MOTHER: I'm going to draw a bucket of water. (*She picks up the bucket and leaves, that is, goes behind the screen.*)

SAÏD (*grimly, with his head down*): I almost got into a fight.

LEILA: The soup'll be ready in half an hour. (*A pause.*) It'll be too salty.

SAÏD (*harshly*): You don't ask me why I almost got into a fight because you know why. (*A pause.*) One day I scraped together all my savings, I added them up, I added all the odds and ends I'd picked up. . . .

LEILA (*with sudden gravity*): Saïd, be quiet.

SAÏD (*continuing, more and more spitefully*): . . . and I put in hours and days of overtime, and I added up again: it didn't come to much. (LEILA *is seized with a violent fit of trembling.*) . . . Then I looked around me, I went over in my mind all the fathers who had daughters. There were loads of them, loads, loads! Dozens, hundreds, thousands . . .

LEILA (*trembling more and more violently, and falling to her knees*): Please, Saïd, be quiet! Please, Lord, please, stop up your ears, don't listen to him!

SAÏD (*with a fresh burst*): . . . hundreds of thousands, but they all, every one of them, asked a few pennies more for the ugliest one they had left. So I got desperate. I still didn't dare think of your father . . .

LEILA (*weeping at* SAÏD'*s feet*): Saïd, my handsome Saïd, be quiet! Lord, Lord God, don't listen to him, it would pain you!

SAÏD: . . . finally, I dared think of him and I was flooded with kindness. I had to receive the ugliest one, and that would be nothing compared to my misfortune, but the cheapest one, and now I have to get into a fight every afternoon with the other farm hands who kid the shirt off me. And when I get home after a day's work, instead of comforting me, you purposely make yourself uglier by crying. (LEILA, *in a squatting, almost crawling position, starts leaving, left.*) Where are you going?

LEILA (*without getting up, without turning around*): To wipe my nose in the garden, to wash away my snot and tears, and to comfort myself in the nettles.

Exit LEILA.

SAÏD (*alone. He undoes one of his puttees and scratches his leg*): And besides, the dough, all that dough I've got to shell out for the whorehouse!

Enter THE MOTHER, *very slowly, leaning to the right, for she is carrying a bucket full of water. She draws herself up when* SAÏD *makes a move to help her.*

THE MOTHER: We'll stint. Drive yourself to the limit of your strength. She, to the limit of hers. We'll see. (*She puts down the bucket.*)
SAÏD: What's she doing in the nettles?
THE MOTHER: Attending to the farm.

We hear the imaginary barnyard sounds which LEILA *is imitating off-stage.* THE MOTHER *doubles up with laughter that mingles with the crowing of cocks and cooing of pigeons.*

SCENE FOUR

The screen—five panels—depicts a field of palmettos. A round, yellow, tissue-paper sun painted on a very blue sky. In front of the parapet, a wheelbarrow (red).

HABIB'S *costume: black trousers, yellow shirt, white sneakers.*
SAÏD'S *costume: as before.*

SIR HAROLD: *forty-five years old. Very manly, to use the language of the colonists. Boots, cork helmet, gloves, switch, riding breeches. He*

tosses back the reins of a horse which is supposed to be behind the
screen. But he too should be highly caricatured: bushy red hair and
eyebrows, big, bristling mustache, red chin, huge freckles, etc. Whenever
he is on-stage, he plays a great deal with his glove and whip.

SIR HAROLD (*to* SAÏD, *who is pushing a wheelbarrow*): Spit in your
   mitts, that keeps your pecker up. (SAÏD *does not move.*)
   Spit, damn it! (*He pronounces "dammt."*)
SAÏD: Spit. (*A pause.*) But on whom, Sir Harold?
SIR HAROLD (*to the horse supposed to be off-stage*): Quiet, Jewel!
HABIB (*mealy-mouthed*): You mustn't be angry with him, Sir
   Harold. He's young. He hasn't been to France yet. He's
   never seen the Eiffel Tower or been to Fontainebleau.
SAÏD: I may be there before long.
SIR HAROLD: Are you planning to leave the country? What
   about your wife? Taking her with you?
HABIB (*roaring with laughter, slaps both his thighs*): That's it,
   that's it, Sir Harold! It's on her you should have told him
   to spit, not in his hands.
SAÏD: Don't listen to him. If I cross the sea, it's to make more
   money. My cousin told me I can get a job and that I'll
   be able to save.
SIR HAROLD (*to the horse supposed to be off-stage*): Quiet, Jewel!
   (*To* SAÏD): Do you need to save money? What for? You
   earn enough to live.
HABIB (*straightening up*): *I* can tell you what for. (*He takes his*
   package of tobacco from his pocket.)   May I light a cigarette,
   Sir Harold? Because it's only when the boss is around
   that I stop for a smoke. Work is work. It's got to be done
   and I can be relied on. (*He rolls a cigarette and lights it.*)
   Yes, I can tell you what for. (*He laughs.*)
SAÏD (*resolutely*): My business . . .
HABIB (*breaking in*): I didn't ask you anything.
SAÏD: You did. In saying it was no fun slaving away with

such a gloomy guy.

HABIB: What about your sighing? Eh? Your sighing? You yawned so much that you swallowed all the birds and there were none left to eat the plant lice. The vines suffered because of your sighing. The vineyards, your vineyards, Sir Harold, are in for trouble.

SAÏD: You know it's summer and the birds are on their way to France! It wasn't me who swallowed them, but you'll accuse me of whatever goes wrong anywhere. And you'll have the nerve to try to read what was on my face. I'm telling you straight from the shoulder.

HABIB (*stubbornly*): I read nothing at all. It was you who spoke. And now I know why you're going to France to work in a coal mine. And I can tell you that you're a disgrace to us all, since Leila's my cousin.

SAÏD: Such a distant one . . . such a distant one . . . that she looks like a bean a hundred feet away.

HABIB: If the distance between her blood and mine were the beans in a bushel laid end to end, she'd still be my cousin, and her shame would cause me a slight—oh, very slight!—feeling of shame.

SAÏD: I'll bring back enough money to buy one. . . .

HABIB: Fine, but what about the other one?

SIR HAROLD (*to the horse, as before*): Quiet, Jewel!

SAÏD: Your cousin?

HABIB: Oh, such a distant one! Anyway, if you like . . . in order to get rid of her, you'll have to pay her father for the shame of the divorce, and shell out, and shell out, and shell out the dough from the mine. (*As if speaking to the horse supposed to be off-stage*): Take it easy, Jewel, nice Jewel! . . . She must be light on her feet. That's an animal for riding at night, when all's asleep. That's the kind of animal you need for such a fine estate: acres here, acres over there, acres to the edge of the sky. (*To* SAÏD):

And you, bringing back dough from France, that's easy to say, but . . .

SIR HAROLD (*in the tone of a jurist*): Unless she gives him a pair of horns during his stay in the mother country. He'd have an excuse.

HABIB (*laughing*): Horns! Oh, Sir Harold, you're pulling his leg! Who'd want to ride her? A fellow would have to be pretty hard up for that. He might jump Saïd, but not his wife.

SIR HAROLD (*to* SAÏD): Is she really as homely as that?

SAÏD (*shyly, lowering his head*): She *is*, Sir Harold.

SIR HAROLD: And you want to cross the sea to be able to pay for a prettier one? But, after all, a pair of thighs is a pair of thighs! (*He roars with laughter and taps his thighs with his switch.*) Ah! ha, ha, ha, ha, those Mohammedans. Poor Saïd! Keep your wife to sew on your buttons, and go pop them in the whorehouse! (*Suddenly he grows impatient. He goes up to* SAÏD. *He spits in his hands and seizes the wheel-barrow.*) God damn it! Like that, I told you. Like that! Didn't your mother ever teach you anything? (*Nervous and irritated, he seems to go back to his horse. To* HABIB): Back to work. (*He leaves as if he were mounting the horse.*)

HABIB: You going already, Sir Harold?

THE GLOVE (*with* SIR HAROLD's *voice*): Not entirely. My glove'll guard you!

A wonderful pigskin glove flies in, directed by a mechanism behind the screen. It remains in the air, as if suspended, in the center of the stage.

SAÏD (*who had bent down*): Was there any need for you to tell him all that?

HABIB (*putting a finger to his lips, then pointing to the glove*): Sh!

SAÏD (*frightened*): Good God! What's in it? His fist?

HABIB: Straw. Packed tight, so as to look as if his fist were

in it. . . . (*A pause.*) And so as to look more dangerous. . . .
(*A pause.*) And to look more real. . . .

SAÏD (*looking at the object*): It looks more beautiful.

HABIB (*sarcastically*): So it does! (*A long silence.*) It's evening,
got to be getting home. (*In a low voice.*) Every finger is
listening with an ear as big as an umbrella. . . . Be
careful! . . . It's evening. (HABIB *tears up the paper sun, rolls
it into a ball and flings it away.*)

SAÏD: Yes, I'm sighing, oh pigskin glove, oh tawny leather
boots, oh sheepskin breeches, I yawn and swallow flocks
of birds, but why make fun of me?

HABIB: Forget about it. (*Looking into the distance.*) Now he's
yelling at Kacem who let out too much water when he
opened the flood gates. He's mounting his mare, he's
plunging into the twilight. (*Looking in front of him, he seems
to be talking to the horse in the distance.*) Jewel! Jewel! A white
hock. White hocks. Mocking eyes. There's a tang in the
air about your body. Are you laughing, Jewel? My
thighs gripping your nice round belly . . . Walk,
Jewel . . . in the moonlight, at a foot pace, Jewel. . . .
(*To* SAÏD): He's stopped thinking about you. He's on his
horse, and on his land.

SAÏD: What you told him leaves traces only in me.

HABIB (*after a silence*): Boujad's farm's going to blaze tonight.
(*Silence.*) What about money for the trip?

SAÏD (*anxiously*): Do you suspect me?

Darkness is coming on.

HABIB (*ironically*): No, no. Not yet. But a man who has the
grandiose idea of crossing the briny deep . . . Eh? You're
not going to swim it?

SAÏD: I'm going to work. (*Shivering.*) It's getting windy.

Both men imitate the sound of the wind, and shiver.

HABIB: How are you going to hoe the beets when the sun goes
    down—with a lantern or a cigarette lighter?
SAÏD (*anxiously*): So you suspect me?

Darkness has set in.

HABIB (*in a clear, very sharp voice*): No. (*A pause.*) I've already
    told you: train yourself to spit in your hands, that'll make
    you seem like a plugger. Things are happening. The
    country has goose flesh. Because of pigskin gloves? We've
    got goose flesh because they no longer give us goose flesh.
    Spit on your hands, Saïd. . . . No stirrups, no bridle, no
    saddle, only my thighs to guide her.
SAÏD: It's blowing hard!

Whirling about as if the wind were sweeping them up, SAÏD *and* HABIB
leave the stage, left. The screen leaves with them, same direction.

SCENE FIVE

*A four-paneled screen in the left corner of the stage represents the front
of the prison: the big door and, on each side, a low, barred window.
Left, a lone palm tree. The time is night.*

TALEB's *costume: green trousers, red jacket worn directly on his naked torso, white shoes.*

THE MOTHER, LEILA, *then* TALEB, *the man who was robbed. They enter from behind the screen in the order indicated. We hear* TALEB *when only* THE MOTHER *is visible.*

TALEB: Plus 9,000 francs that the flood cost me, that makes 17,203 francs I'm out of pocket. The flood picked the wrong time. . . . It's as if it had meant to aggravate Saïd's case. If he'd stolen my jacket when the harvest was good, it would have been different. (*Forcefully.*) Lousy luck, the flood's lousy luck, the theft's lousy luck, and Saïd's mixed up in my lousy luck.

THE MOTHER (*without turning around*): To think they set up prisons stone by stone, at the tops of hills, and that you have to keep going up to get to the gate. Ah, my stick!

TALEB: In a way, he's not an ordinary thief. I was saving up. I was just about to buy my motor bike. The floods and Saïd at the same time. I've been plagued by two-headed bad luck, with four hands and twenty fingers.

THE MOTHER (*out of breath, wiping her face with a rag which she throws to* LEILA): Here, wipe yourself. It's the rag for the asses of the pots. (*She laughs.*) Give yourself a good wipe.

LEILA (*to* TALEB): Not 17,000, since the 8,000 was given back. Saïd was honest. He could have said he'd lost it, or that you'd stolen it back from him.

TALEB: It's you who defend him! If he stole the dough from my red jacket that was under the fig tree, it was to pay for the trip, so as to take a job—or rather to slave—in France, to save up and buy himself another wife.

LEILA: So he says. But instead of leaving me, he got caught and was grilled and thrown into prison up the hill.

TALEB: I withdrew my complaint. He'll be . . .

THE MOTHER: Withdrew it? (*Threateningly.*) Your complaints are complaints for all eternity.

TALEB: I've spread word all through the village that he did the right thing. My jacket's red, and it could easily have been mistaken for his in the twilight.

THE MOTHER: People will continue to know he's a thief. And when I fight with the village women, the bitches, they'll be able to insult me and make up millions of things about Saïd and me.

LEILA: And me too?

THE MOTHER (*shrugging*): Nothing more can be said about you. Idiot.

TALEB: What things?

THE MOTHER: They'll say first that he's a thief, therefore that his feet stink, and his teeth and his mouth. That he sucks his thumb, that he talks to himself when he's alone. . . . About me they'll say what there is to say, that I spawned a thief.

TALEB: You'll find lots of other insults to fling back at them.

THE MOTHER: Not so easy. A just insult can take your breath away, can pluck your tongue out, can dim your sight. What do you do then? (*She draws herself up. Proudly.*) I know—dazzle them with my shame. Ah, if I were Saïd! . . .

TALEB: You . . .

THE MOTHER (*interrupting him*): Yes! They'd fall to their knees. Standing upright, with my legs spread, I'd unbutton my fly. But all I have is my insults. If I falter, the other women run looking for new ones.

TALEB: You'll outspeed them with your rage.

THE MOTHER (*threateningly*): Go away! Get the hell out of here! You're trying to win me by flattery.

LEILA (*to* THE MOTHER): I'll help you. I've got a cartload of filth in reserve.

THE MOTHER (*shrugging*): Idiot.

LEILA: Every night I learn new insults. They can be helpful.

THE MOTHER: So you don't sleep?

TALEB: I first accused the Ben Ammar boy.

THE MOTHER (*wild with rage*): A fine how-do-you-do! The whole Ben Ammar family on our necks! Clear out or I'll break my stick on your back!

TALEB *leaves.* THE MOTHER *and* LEILA *sit down by the door of the prison. A long silence, broken by* LEILA's *sighs.*

THE MOTHER (*laughing*): You always give the chickens too much grain. I've told you, half a potful's enough.

LEILA: That's not much, you know.

THE MOTHER (*more gently*): Let them go steal elsewhere.

LEILA (*very gravely*): I thought of that, but do you think it's easy to get under the netting around the yards? And with the roosters all acting like cops with clubs and stony beaks?

THE MOTHER: All you have to do is teach them. Let them go steal. Don't forget that it's on account of you we're thieves. Our chickens'll be thieves too.

LEILA (*astonished*): On account of me?

THE MOTHER (*laughing*): Of your ugliness.

LEILA (*very calmly*): That's so. I'll do what I can about the chickens. There's one I've noticed in particular, the black one, she's more depraved than the others. If only she could teach the white chickens how to go about it!

THE MOTHER: And don't forget to go cut the reeds.

A long silence. Then the two women hum a kind of chant. Finally SAÏD *appears, carrying a bundle on his shoulder. He greets neither his wife nor his mother. The two women stand up.*

THE MOTHER: Did you remember to bring back the old blanket?

SAÏD: I did. (*They walk without changing place, while the screen moves back into the left wing. Finally they stop.*) Tomorrow I'm taking a job at the phosphate mine.

A pause.

THE MOTHER: What about the money?

A pause.

SAÏD: By money order.

THE MOTHER (*stopping in order to examine* SAÏD): It's *really* true that you've changed.

SAÏD: It's the lack of air.

They start walking again in silence.

SAÏD (*to* LEILA): Leila.

LEILA (*she stops*): Yes, Saïd.

SAÏD: Take off your veil so I can look at you.

LEILA (*turning to him*): Don't bother, Saïd. I'm as homely as ever.

THE MOTHER (*laughing*): Let's get a move on. I feel someone calling me. (*She continues on her way.*)

LEILA (*gently*): Do you? (*Silence.*) Beneath a spot of moon, do you want to see me, Saïd?

SAÏD (*sternly*): No.

They start walking. They take a few steps.

LEILA (*following rather far behind*): I'm all alone.

THE MOTHER: So what? Do as I do. Learn to recognize the

different varieties of forest trees in the darkness by the sound of the wind in the branches. It's a pastime, and it'll make you more refined. . . . If not your eyes, in any case your ears . . .

SAÏD *and* LEILA *leave after going behind the screen.* THE MOTHER *remains on the stage platform, rear, where the screen for Scene Six will appear.*

SCENE SIX

A five-paneled screen, spread open against the back wall, represents the square of an Arab village: a painted palm tree, the grave of a marabout.

Five open umbrellas are resting upside down in front of the screen. A blazing sun is painted on a very blue sky. All the women leave, at the end, each protecting herself from the sun with an umbrella.

All the women—except THE MOTHER—*are wearing black dresses. On their heads, black veils. Three women are on-stage at the beginning:* CHIGHA, KADIDJA *and* NEDJMA.

CHIGHA *is about forty years old;* KADIDJA, *about sixty; and* NEDJMA *about twenty.*

CHIGHA (*with mincing steps she walks from the right side of the stage toward the left wing. She cries out*): Hurry up! If we're late, there'll be no flies left! (*Humming.*) The flies! The flies! The flies! . . .

KADIDJA: Has anyone ever heard, even in winter, of a dead body without flies? A corpse without flies is a dismal corpse. Flies are part of mourning. (*Her black stocking is falling down; she lifts up her skirt to fasten the stocking to her garter.*)

CHIGHA (*laughing*): Then my house has been in mourning a long time. Funerals are probably going on there all day long. The flies are running away with the place. Flies in the cellar, flies on the ceiling, and their droppings on my skin . . .

NEDJMA (*with visible disgust*): If the foreigners despise us, it's because there are still women like you. They invented Ajax in order to scrape the filth off us. Their women stay . . .

CHIGHA: . . . in warm water for ten hours. Stewing for ten hours. I go to the bath house too . . . to walk my white dogs in the dust afterwards. . . .

NEDJMA (*picking up an umbrella to protect herself from the sun*): Later on *I'll* live Italian-style. There'll be neither flies nor cockroaches in *my* room. . . .

CHIGHA (*laughing*): There're flies, roaches, and spiders at my place! But mostly flies. There'll always be a little something for them to eat at the corner of the kids' eyes—I bring kids up for that—and under their noses. I give 'em a smack from time to time, around ten in the morning, a wallop at four in the afternoon! They bawl and snivel and our flies have a blowout. (*With her tongue she seems to be licking with relish the snot she pretends is flowing from her nose.*)

NEDJMA (*disgusted*): And your man . . .

CHIGHA: No, with him it's on the elbows and fingers that there's always a little scab. And me . . .

KADIDJA: Be quiet, you two idiots. There'll be flies. I hear them from here. All the same, the sun is setting. But it'll be here, nevertheless, the black flag. (*She speaks to someone behind the screen*): Well, shake a leg. Think of the flies there'll be.

A VOICE (*of someone who is squatting behind an umbrella*): Every time I go to a funeral you tell me to hurry up because of the flies, and when the body's lowered they're all already there. I've counted them.

HABIBA *appears. Twenty years old. She shelters herself from the sun beneath a black umbrella.*

HABIBA: They buzz around the hole as loud as a tin Lizzy, or as my man when he gives me a workout. Shall we go?

CHIGHA: Wait'll I take a piss. (*She runs and disappears behind the screen. A pause.*)

NEDJMA (*dreamily*): . . . I saw another one, a blue one, sky-blue, like sky-blue wool. That's the one I'll get. (*A pause.*) I'll go and empty it every morning on the far side of the garden.

THE MOTHER—*who was on the second stage platform—appears.*

KADIDJA (*firmly planted on her legs*): You haven't come to mourn the dead?

THE MOTHER (*astounded for a moment*): I'm a mourner, I've come.

KADIDJA: Not with us.

THE MOTHER: Why not? What have I done?

KADIDJA: Your son and daughter-in-law are in jail. . . .

THE MOTHER: No. She got out this morning.

KADIDJA: In any case, she's a thief. She talks to nettles in

ditches. She tries to domesticate them. The nettles answer.
Your son's a thief. And you, you profit from the chickens,
cabbage, figs, coal, kerosene, and margarine that he steals.
You can't come with us.

THE MOTHER: If a man in one of your families or a woman in
one of your families had died on his or her cot, I wouldn't
be here to mourn, ladies, but to sing. The man who's being
buried today isn't like the other dead. Nor is he the son
of any one of you, and that's why I've come to annoy you.
I know more about funerals than anyone else—I manu-
facture little ones to amuse myself. The flies know me too,
just as I know *them*, all of them, by their names. (*A pause.*)
And as for nettles, when Leila talks to them she converses
with our family.

KADIDJA: You're a family of thieves. Here in the village we
have a right to dispense our own justice. We're among
ourselves. You won't follow the corpse.

THE MOTHER: Who'll prevent me from coming?

KADIDJA: The corpse.

Re-enter CHIGHA.

THE MOTHER: A corpse doesn't impress me. (*To* CHIGHA): Rich
as you are, you still relieve yourself behind a fence. Can't
you get someone to buy you a sky-blue pot that you can
empty every morning?

NEDJMA (*shouting*): It's mine!

KADIDJA: That'll do. Let's get going. (*To* THE MOTHER): Stay
there!

THE MOTHER: Ah, if I were Saïd, I'd shut up that mouth, that
toothless black mouth of yours!

KADIDJA (*ironically*): You're *not* Saïd? Then who *is* Saïd? And
where *is* this Saïd?

THE MOTHER: He just left—hurrah!—for court and he's going

back to jail. And he'll stay there as long as necessary to
pay for what he'll steal from you when he gets out, and
as long as necessary for me to set at your heels the pack
of dogs gathering in my belly. As for the corpse, I no
longer want . . .

KADIDJA (*to the other women*): Well? What do you say? (*After a
brief hesitation, the three women shake their heads.*) You see,
it's not I who speak, but public opinion.

THE MOTHER (*solemnly*): What about the corpse, what does the
corpse say?

KADIDJA (*to the other women*): You, the corpse, what does he
say? Listen! Listen carefully. What does he say? (*The
women seem to be listening. Then they shake their heads and with
their hands make a sign meaning "No."*) Did you hear? The
voice of the corpse has gone by. . . .

THE MOTHER: I'm telling you . . .

KADIDJA (*interrupting her brutally*): If I'd questioned the dogs—
you hear me—the dogs in your belly that are getting
ready to bite us, they'd have answered no! The dogs, the
mares, the chickens, the ducks, the broom, the ball of
wool would have said no!

THE MOTHER: If the dogs talk like you, you talk like them.
(*The three women make as if to rush at her; she withdraws to
the back of the stage.*) All right. Very well, ladies. You're
decent. . . . You're decent, and there's nothing to be said
against that. Maybe the corpse answered as you say, but
I want to be sure, and I'll go question it tomorrow, at
noon. Today it's too hot, and I've had my ration of flies
with those that stream out of your mud-wiped mugs.

*She is about to leave, but as she is downstage, left, the way is barred
by* KADIDJA *and the other women. It is they who will walk off,
backwards.*

KADIDJA: Don't move. (*To the other women*): As for you, I expect
you to mourn properly. And to moan good long moans,
loud ones. Vibrant. Without breathing. It's not an
ordinary corpse. . . .

HABIBA: What's so special about him, now that he's dead?

THE MOTHER *laughs out loud.*

KADIDJA (*severely*): We've been ordered to mourn a corpse that's
more than another corpse. We mourn and we moan.

Walking backwards, the four women go upstage, leaving THE MOTHER
alone, downstage, left.

CHIGHA: A good reason. When my son Abdallah refuses to give
me an explanation, I feel unhappy for the moment, but I
get over it. . . . (THE MOTHER *again bursts out laughing.*)
And on the whole, I find it very beautiful to be ordered
to rejoice or mourn without knowing why. My men want
my moans and my laughter to be beautiful. Since I have
no sorrow—it's they who bear it—and no joy, I can
attend to my work . . . nice and calmly. . . .

THE MOTHER (*suddenly infuriated, facing the audience*): Nice and
calmly! Get the hell out of here! Go accompany calmness
to the cemetery. But let me tell you something—that this
evening, when night comes, if you don't come out, I'll go
limping, bent double, beneath the moon, into each of your
houses. And if you're drowsing, I'll compel you to steal
cutlets and chickens in your dreams every night. I'll recite
a hundred and twenty-seven insults a hundred and twenty-
seven times, and each insult will be so beautiful, ladies,
that it'll make you gleam. . . .

The women have disappeared. THE MOTHER *turns about and becomes aware that they have gone. For a moment she is disconcerted. Then she walks around the stage, seeming to contain within herself a great force. Then, suddenly, planted on her bent legs, with her hands on her thighs, she unlooses, in the direction of the right wing, into which the women disappeared, a torrent of barks that seem to come from a pack of dogs, while* LEILA, *who has entered, barks with her.*

They stop for a few seconds, and we hear, from the wing by which the women left, the mooing of cows. THE MOTHER *and* LEILA *resume their barking, then stop again. Then, again, in the distance, the mooing and the sound of galloping hooves.* THE MOTHER *and* LEILA *are still looking into the wings. Then their gazes shift and rise up to the flies. We still hear the galloping of the herd. It grows faint. Below, where the screen was, a huge moon appears. All is silent.* THE MOTHER *turns around and, seeing* LEILA, *starts barking at her, and the two women are suddenly dogs about to devour each other.*

*The moon shifts gradually and disappears. Its place is taken by a new screen (taller than the preceding one) which enters quietly on a kind of black platform that emerges from the right wing. The scene that will take place in front of it will therefore be played about seven feet from the floor. The screen representing the square goes back into the wing. The two women (*THE MOTHER *and* LEILA*) keep barking. The upper screen is brightly lit.* THE MOTHER *and* LEILA *are in semi-darkness.*

SCENE SEVEN

A whitewashed four-paneled screen, in which a window is cut out. Behind, the sun. In front of the screen, a huge Koran (title in Roman letters) on a small table. Above the Koran, a lighted hanging lamp.

Costumes:
THE WOMAN: *a green silk dress.*
THE FLUTE PLAYER: *yellow trousers. Barefooted and bare-chested. A blue cap.*
THE MAN WHO PISSED: *black trousers, green shoes, pink jacket.*
THE POLICEMAN: *white uniform.*
THE CADI: *traditional Algerian costume, sky-blue silk. Pale pink turban.*

THE FLUTE PLAYER: . . . so it's not exactly begging. I'm not destitute.

THE POLICEMAN (*joyously, with a cluck of his tongue and snap of his fingers*): Ah! (*He utters this "Ah!" as if it were a deliverance, ceremoniously.*) Every police order, the most modest circular, the lowest-ranking policeman, far off, beyond seas and mountains, all and everything delegated me to intervene, for all and everything felt irritation. (*Accusingly.*) He was the shame of the street, Your Excellency. At times he played two flutes, one in each nostril.

THE FLUTE PLAYER (*defiantly*): As one plays the violin on two strings, or the typewriter with two hands. A policeman —and yet I respect your profession—cannot understand. But you, Your Excellency, God who is within you will understand me. It took me two years to learn to play the flute properly with my nostrils. If every beggar can do as much, then let me be condemned for begging.

THE POLICEMAN: To the passers-by it was as disturbing to hear his hardwood flute, which perforated his nose, as to see a bare bone jutting from a thigh. Since he caused discomfort for the purpose of collecting money, he was begging. (*Sharply.*) Our function is to suppress begging in public places. . . .

THE CADI (*very gently, but in a trembling voice*): And was what he was playing beautiful?

THE FLUTE PLAYER: The main thing is, it's hard to play. And I've barely got my number into shape. I practice every day in the empty lot. . . .

THE CADI: Is there an empty lot?

THE FLUTE PLAYER: For the needs of the cause.

THE CADI (*very patiently, very gently, and with slight astonishment*): Can you put a flute into your mouth without its bothering you?

THE POLICEMAN's *impatience is very visible.*

THE FLUTE PLAYER: Yes, Your Excellency.

THE CADI (*interested*): Is your breath strong enough to make it vibrate?

THE FLUTE PLAYER: Yes, Your Excellency.

THE CADI (*his voice still trembling*): You therefore sought only difficulty?

THE FLUTE PLAYER: Yes, Your Excellency.

THE CADI: Without thereby desiring more beauty?

THE FLUTE PLAYER: For the first time, the breath that comes out of the two holes of a dirty nose has modulated the air of a hymn, or of a . . . song, or of a . . . melody, or, if you like, of a slow waltz, has imitated the rippling of a stream and the sighing of wind in the branches. I have a nose that's as noble as your mouth. Thanks to my labor, my nose is a harp, yours is only . . .

Suddenly LEILA *comes hopping in, right, howling like an injured dog and pursued by* THE MOTHER, *who is barking fiercely. Outstripped by her daughter-in-law,* THE MOTHER *takes a stone from her pocket and throws it at* LEILA, *who has disappeared. We hear, off-stage, the shattering of a window pane.* THE MOTHER *emerges cautiously.*

THE CADI (*looking through an imaginary window*): Breaking a window pane! Ten days in the jug. (*To* THE FLUTE PLAYER): Go. Go play the double nose-flute. May God punish himself if I'm wrong. (*To the Arab who is approaching*): Your turn.

Exit THE FLUTE PLAYER. *The Arab approaches.*

THE POLICEMAN (*pompously, as before*): Proudly—for there was pride in his posture—proudly he pissed against a young laurel at the edge of the soccer field. Proud, as I myself am as soon as I'm against a wall. . . .

THE CADI (*to* THE POLICEMAN): I've got terrible stage fright. (*To the Arab*): Pissed? Can you tell me why?

THE MAN WHO PISSED: I had to.

THE CADI: But why against that shrub tree?

THE MAN WHO PISSED: It was there.

THE CADI (*interested*): Right now, do you have to?

THE MAN WHO PISSED: No, Your Excellency, not right now.

THE CADI (*at first, as if relieved; as he continues speaking, his voice becomes firmer*): It so happens you don't have to piss, otherwise it's down my leg that your water would be flowing. But I could punish you without bringing you to trial. One kills those who kill. If you poured out on me, I'd wet you too, and with a stiffer jet than yours. We could tilt at each other with lances of warm water, and you'd be beaten, because while waiting for God to enter me and inspire me, I drank a big jugful of mint water. But relieving yourself against the shapely right leg of a beautiful young laurel! Three or four leaves of which are likely to be yellowed! (*To* THE SECOND POLICEMAN): take him out and piss on his feet.

THE POLICEMAN *has the Arab taken out, but he himself remains.* THE WOMAN *approaches.*

THE CADI (*a little more violently*): Step up quickly, and tell me quickly what you did if you want me to judge you before God goes away.

THE WOMAN: I didn't do anything, Your Excellency.

THE CADI (*to* THE WOMAN): God's shoving off. If you want to be judged by him—therefore with a remnant of kindness —help me. Tell me what judgment you want, but tell me fast.

THE WOMAN (*very quickly*): Ten blows with a stick, Your Excellency.

THE CADI (*to* THE POLICEMAN): Give 'er fifteen.

Exit THE WOMAN. SAÏD *enters and approaches.*

THE CADI (*putting his hand to his forehead*): God has lit out, skedaddled, scrammed. God has gone away. (*He grows more and more irritated.*) He comes, he goes, I wonder where?

Into another head? Into a wasp in the sun? Into the bend of a road? Into a pot to add a little fat? In any case, he's cleared out of my Cadi's head. My stage fright's gone and my voice is no longer trembling.

SAÏD: My name is Saïd, Your Excellency.

THE CADI (*very ill-humoredly*): I've stopped judging. Go away.

SAÏD: I've stolen, Your Excellency. You have to sentence me.

THE CADI: With what? (*He strikes his head.*) It's empty in there.

SAÏD: I beg you!

THE POLICEMAN (*snickering*): Stolen. His speciality, as you know, is workmen's jackets hanging from the branches of almond trees or lying on a clump. This character, Your Excellency, is a snake in the grass. It's from neither here nor there. It steals without remorse. And yet, as if he were a rich man, he's an only son. (*To* SAÏD): From what jacket was it?

SAÏD: This one and that one.

THE POLICEMAN: I know. Doesn't matter. The thing is, to steal. Without being choosy. As unjust as a railway accident. Luckily we're sharp-eyed. (*Roaring.*) Eyes wide open in the leaves or bushes, and never fazed.

SAÏD: All I'm asking is to serve my sentence.

THE CADI (*with a gesture, he stops* THE POLICEMAN, *who tries to put a word in*): One would think you were getting panicky, that you feel a time coming when everything will change. . . . Is the death of Si Slimane preying on your mind? But of what use will it be to me to judge you?

SAÏD: The wrong I've done should . . .

THE CADI: You fool. It'll be of use to you. After the judgment and after the penalty you'll be transformed—a tiny little bit—but what about me, if after the judgment, if after the penalty, I remain the same . . . .

SAÏD: Try, you'll see. . . .

THE POLICEMAN (*to* THE CADI): To serve his sentence, he said,

to serve his sentence. That's easy to say. There's more to
it than that. (*To* SAÏD): This morning, at eight o'clock,
this morning, order of release. Your wife got out of prison
this morning. . . .

THE CADI (*to* THE POLICEMAN): Go piss on the foot of the laurel.

THE POLICEMAN: But . . . Your Excell . . .

THE CADI (*out of patience*): Go piss. In the shrubbery or under
the branches, but go.

Exit THE POLICEMAN. THE CADI *looks at* SAÏD *curiously and goes up
to him.*

THE CADI (*gently*): I'm fed up. Think of the nonsensical prob-
lems laid before me. I'm judge of a village where ghastly
crimes are probably being committed every minute—
(*Anxiously.*) or is anything a crime?—and the world offers
up to God only one or two charming trifles. I'm fed up,
and my head is all the heavier for being empty.

SAÏD: Do it anyway. I'll be satisfied. I'm not proud, and I'm
not asking that God go to the trouble of opening a prison
door for me. A Cadi can do it.

THE CADI (*gravely*): If all I had to do was open a door and shut
it again, I would. But I need a reason. In order to find
it, I'd either have to look for it, and I'm tired, or I'd have
to have done exactly what you did. . . . The long and
short of it is that you're the only one capable of knowing.
Either God judges you—he knows all, but he's no longer
here—or else you judge yourself and I serve no purpose.

SAÏD: You're forgetting one thing: that you're paid to open
and shut the door of the jail. (*A pause.*) I can't serve
myself.

THE CADI (*perplexed*): No, of course . . . and yet, that's what'll
have to be done. . . .

SAÏD: I'd no longer be taken seriously.

THE CADI: That's to fear. But you're asking me to do a grave thing. . . . You steal often. I spend my time sending you to jail. You sense something. . . . You know that by going to jail you escape the obligations that are now going. . . . Nothing's sacred to you. Not even loose change. Saïd, I could play a dirty trick on you: I could acquit you of each of your crimes. I'd deliver sentence in the name of God and the people. . . .

SAÏD: You'd be killing me.

THE CADI: I see very well—I'm no dope—what you gain by each new condemnation, I see, vaguely, where you're heading, but what about me, to what does each new condemnation lead *me?*

LEILA, *below, limps across the stage, barking. Blackout.*

SCENE EIGHT

A five-paneled screen representing the cemetery. Right, a cypress tree. Painted on the screen, center, a tombstone. In the dark sky, a crescent moon and a constellation. At the foot of the screen, a small watering can.

THE MOUTH'*s costume: a vaguely Arab costume* (*white*).

THE MOTHER (*speaking to invisible women*): From where you are

. . . stop! Stay where you are! You'll be able to hear from where you are. (*She goes to the tombstone and makes out the inscription.*) Si Slimane. It's his grave. (*Turning to the left wing.*) Come here! Come along, here! Or are you really completely useless? Are you deaf? Too old, perhaps?

Enter MADANI, *an old Arab.*

MADANI: If you're not satisfied with me, you still have time to go choose another Mouth. (*A slight pause.*) But don't insult me.

THE MOTHER: This is no time for getting angry. I wanted the oldest and clumsiest Mouth, because I'm honest. If I'd brought along a fresh, pink Mouth with nice white teeth, I'd have given the impression of trying to influence the dead man. Stand there. (MADANI *stands at the left of the grave.*) I've picked you to be the dead man's Mouth. I realize it must be full of earth and roots and gravel, but try to articulate clearly the words of the dead man, not your own.

MADANI: When a dead man agrees to speak, he has something awful to say. It's he who'll speak.

THE MOTHER: Is it time?

MADANI (*looking at his wrist watch*): Right now.

THE MOTHER (*facing the women, who are still invisible*): And on your hills, amidst the odor of wild thyme, try, try, old women and maidens, to stop your cackling. It won't be long now. The dead man has something to say. (*To* MADANI): I have coffee in a thermos bottle. For later. I can leave you for a moment, if you have any preparations to make.

MADANI (*squatting very slowly*): I don't mind your presence. The hardest thing is to take leave of myself. He'll come and replace me.

THE MOTHER (*a little anxiously*): Oh? . . . And . . . if you take leave of yourself, where do you go?

MADANI (*continuing to squat*): It depends . . . whether I start with a rapid movement, or one that's too slow. If I have time, I visit my olive trees, or the Museum of the Veterans Hospital. . . . Leave me. (*He lies down completely and, after a silence, he calls softly.*) Si Slimane? . . . Si Slimane? . . . Slimane, are you there? . . . (*He listens.*) Are you there? Yes . . . Yes? . . . Who's answering? Is it you, Si Slimane? . . . It's me here. . . . It's your Mouth. . . . It's your poor unhappy Mouth full of earth and gravel and roots that has to answer. Do you recognize me? . . . What, you don't remember? It's I who uttered all your remarks when you were alive. . . . (*A silence.*) What remarks? Why, all of them . . . everything you said . . . what you once said to the road inspector . . . you remember? . . . Ah, you see . . . What you said?

A pause.

THE MOTHER: Doesn't he recognize you?

MADANI: Let me do my job. I've got to warm him up. (*Speaking to the dead man*): What you said to the road inspector. . . . It was raining that day. You said to him: "I'm going to the shed to get out of the rain. When it stops, I'll take the plans to the architect!" (*A pause.*) Ah, you're with me now! Good. So you recognize me. . . . (*A pause.*) My smell? . . . Here . . . (*He breathes on the grave.*) Is that the smell of your mouth? It is! Ah, well then, let's go. Saïd's mother has come to find out. (*He stands up and, facing* THE MOTHER, *he speaks commandingly, without moving.*) You, speak. Question me. I'm the Mouth. You've come to hear me. Speak up. What's on your mind?

The light is focused on MADANI *and* THE MOTHER *who, face to face, look each other up and down.*

THE MOTHER (*dubiously*): Are you Si Slimane's Mouth?

THE MOUTH (*forcefully*): I am.

THE MOTHER: Then where were you born?

THE MOUTH: Born at Bou Caniz. Died at Aïn Amar.

THE MOTHER (*taken aback for a moment*): Very well. And . . . your wound, where were you wounded?

THE MOUTH: Two bullets in my chest. One remained.

THE MOTHER: Very well . . . And . . . at exactly what time did you die?

THE MOUTH (*impatiently and with authority*): Enough. I've said enough. What do you want to know?

THE MOTHER (*same tone*): As you like. I know you're not easy to deal with, but neither am I. It seems you've ordered the women of the village to keep me from mourning. Is that true?

THE MOUTH (*hesitantly*): I didn't want you at my funeral.

THE MOTHER (*angrily*): Where did Saïd come from, my belly or yours? And is my belly any different from those of the other women? Am I a different kind of mother from the other women?

THE MOUTH: I was dead and not yet buried. I was still part of the village. I had the same itching in my hair, on the soles of my feet, on my back, as the men and women of the village. . . .

THE MOTHER (*uneasily*): And now . . . now that you're unable to scratch yourself?

THE MOUTH: Much less. Despite all the weight of the earth, I feel much lighter. I'm about to evaporate—it's a good thing you didn't wait and that you came this evening— all my juice is seeping into the veins of the cork trees and the heads of lettuce. I'm wandering through my land, and you, I merge you with everyone else. . . .

THE MOTHER (*a tremendous scream*): Ah! Ah! Ah!

THE MOUTH: . . . and a little of the dirt you keep between your toes comes from my decay. . . .

THE MOTHER (*victoriously turning toward the wing*): You bitches, you band of bitches, you hear him, you hear how the dead man talks to me? (*To* THE MOUTH): In the North, in the East, in the South, toward Aïn Zefra, toward China and toward the sea, everywhere, all about us, the night is rising, Slimane, is swelling up with hills, and on the slopes of the hills that are watching us a thousand—a hundred thousand—females are expecting to see you pluck yourself, tear yourself from the earth like a beet to insult me. But you . . . you're willing . . . you're willing to let me mourn. . . . Are you? Do you recognize that I'm no different from the other women? . . .

THE MOUTH (*sharply*): Yes and no.

THE MOTHER: That's clear, but I didn't mean that I was a women like them . . . (*Pointing to the wings.*) like those there. I said that I too feed on what rots beneath the earth. . . .

THE MOUTH: You're rotting above it . . . according to what people say. . . .

THE MOTHER (*laughing*): Does that mean you and I are fermenting in the same juice? Is that it?

THE MOUTH: In any case, I wonder why you're so bent on mourning me?

THE MOTHER: Oh, I assure you, it's not the grief your death causes me that would make me sing and weep. Those ladies chased me away from a ceremony. I don't give a damn about them or the ceremony, but I swore to myself I'd outsmart them. They're watching and waiting—the bitches!—waiting for me to be put to shame! They're saying to themselves: kicked out by the living, she's going to be kicked out again by the dead.

THE MOUTH: And what would it matter to you, being kicked out by the dead?

THE MOTHER (*taken aback for a moment*): Ah, because you're linked up, if I gather correctly . . . you haven't forgotten, beneath your gravel, that you were once alive and that you were on friendly terms with so-and-so or so-and-so. . . .

THE MOUTH (*obstinately*): And what would it matter to you, being kicked out by the dead?

THE MOTHER: And that your funeral is also part of your life as a living man! And that you want someone worthy to be a fourth at bridge!

THE MOUTH: And what would it matter to you, being kicked out by the dead?

THE MOTHER: If you have nothing else to say to me, good night. . . .

THE MOUTH (*furiously*): It was you who had the rudeness to come and wake me up, to unearth me in the middle of the night. I've been listening to you and letting you talk. . . .

THE MOTHER: I came as a friend.

THE MOUTH (*severely*): You came puffed with pride. Mother of a thief and of an ugly, stupid, thieving daughter-in-law. Does their sordid sordidness stick to your skin? No, it *is* your skin, stretched across your poor bones. What strolls through the streets of the village is a cloak of sordidness stretched over solid bones, though . . . (*He snickers.*) not so solid. The village doesn't want to put up with you any more, but do the dead? Ah, the dead, you say, approve of you and condemn those ladies?

THE MOTHER (*curtly*): I hoped so.

THE MOUTH (*snickering*): The dead, to be sure, are the last resort. The living spit in your face, but the dead envelop you in their big black, or white, wings. And protected by the wings, you could flout those who go afoot? But those who walk the earth will be inside it before long. They're the same. . . .

THE MOTHER (*interrupting him*): I don't want to know anything about what you've become. It's with the one who was alive that I wanted to have dealings. And if you don't want me to mourn, say so now, I'm chilly. . . .

THE MOUTH: Don't try to play on my feelings. Your pride cuts you off from the living, it won't win you the love of the dead. We're the official bondsmen of the living. (*A pause.*) At midnight! Disturbing me at such an hour! Recalling me to weary life! Go find the women, go, and the men of the village. Have it out among yourselves.

THE MOTHER: I'll hold my own. (*She puts her hands on her hips.*) I refuse to leave Saïd and Leila in the lurch—I say that only to you, in the darkness of the cemetery, because they, both of them, often get on my nerves—and I refuse not to mourn you.

THE MOUTH (*angrily*): What if I don't want you to?

THE MOTHER (*same tone*): And what if, just to spite you, in spite of those ladies and in spite of you, I began mourning you?

THE MOUTH: And what if I really rose up from my grave, from my hole . . .

THE MOTHER (*frightened*): Would you dare? . . . (*Then she pulls herself together.*) Would you dare, you, to disgrace me like that? In front of those ladies listening in? I don't know and don't want to know who murdered you, but you deserved to be murdered, by a knife or a bayonet, for daring to threaten an old woman. I came in anger, Si Slimane. It was anger—or, if you like, rage—that carried me in its arms, all the way to you, rage and rage only.

THE MOUTH: I wonder why you've come to question a dead man?

THE MOTHER: Anger! I've told you. Brought by anger. Where?

If not amidst the graves?

THE MOUTH: You weary me. Your anger is stronger . . .

THE MOTHER: Than your death?

THE MOUTH: No. But go away. It's too hard talking to a living creature as . . . as living as you. Ah . . . if only you were . . .

THE MOTHER: On the brink of the grave? Of yours, yes, not of mine.

THE MOUTH (*suddenly tired*): No, no, not even that. But . . . a little . . . only a tiny bit sick. But there you are, yelling, gesticulating . . . (*He shrugs.*) . . . wanting, for your own purposes, to bring a dead man back to life. (*Yawning.*) It's hard enough to do on important occasions. . . .

THE MOTHER (*suddenly humble*): Wouldn't you like me, on the Q.T., to mourn you here, beneath the moon?

THE MOUTH (*yawning more and more*): No, not even in the hollow of my ear. (*A pause. In a weary voice.*) Would you like me to tell you a little what death is like? What life is like there? . . .

THE MOTHER: That doesn't interest me.

THE MOUTH (*wearier and wearier*): What one purrs there . . .

THE MOTHER: Not tonight. Some day, if I have time, I'll come back and look into it more closely. Live your death, I'll live my life. . . . You really don't want me to . . . mourn?

THE MOUTH: No. (*A pause.*) I'm too weary. (MADANI *suddenly collapses with sleep.*)

THE MOTHER (*clasping her hands and crying out*): Si Slimane! (*She draws close, looks at him, then pushes him with her foot, disgustedly.*) Snoring away! It's obvious you haven't been among the dead very long. Unable to make a Mouth talk more than three minutes. Just long enough to tell me I belong neither here nor there, on neither this side nor the other. (*She laughs.*) I was right yesterday not to mourn such a fresh, such a weak corpse. (*She takes the watering can, sprinkles the supposed mound a little, then, dancing and humming, tamps the earth, shrugging.*) Well, old boy, are you visiting the Museum of the Veterans Hospital? (*She turns around and is about to leave the stage, but she stops short, as if astounded.*) The skunks! The sluts! The bitches! The hills have all spread their sails, and with them have rigged out the females who were spying on us. Gone! Amidst the smell of jasmin and thyme. Gone where? In a band, behind the walls, to thicken the mystery? And the night's left lying flat. Beneath the sky. Flat. The bitches, they didn't have the guts to remain standing. In spite of their woolen shawls, they went back home. I'm all alone and the night's flat . . . (*With sudden solemnity.*) But no, the night has risen, it's swelled up like the teats of a sow . . . from a hundred thousand hills . . . the murderers are descending. . . . The sky's no dope, the sky's camouflaging them. . . .

MADANI (*awakening*): Could you make me a cup of coffee?

THE MOTHER: But actually . . . why did I come? He's dead, but why? (*To* MADANI): Have your Mocha, old thing!

SCENE NINE

The screen (four panels) represents a rampart. At the foot of the rampart, a three-legged table. On the table, a half-burnt-out candle.

LEILA *is alone. Near her, a big tin dishpan. From under her skirt she takes several objects which she lays on the table or hooks to the wall. She speaks to the objects.* THE GENDARME *is wearing a two-pointed cocked hat and white gloves. He has a big black mustache.*

LEILA (*taking out a cheese grater*): Hello! . . . I don't bear grudges. You scraped the skin of my belly, and I say hello to you. . . . Your life will be different. . . . This is the Mother's house. And Saïd's. You won't have much to do, we never put cheese into the noodles. . . . To keep you busy I'll scrape the callus on the sole of my foot. (*She hangs the grater on the wall. She fumbles under her skirt and takes out a lamp, with a shade, which she places on the table.*) What'll I do with a lamp, since there's no electricity at the foot of the ramparts, in the ruins? . . . Well, dear lamp, you'll be able to rest in our house. . . . Always being used . . . makes one bitter. . . . (*She fumbles again under her skirt and takes out a glass, which almost slips from her hands.*) Stop being an ass, or I'll break you! . . . Break you, you hear me . . . break you. (*A pause.*) And then what'll you be? Bits of glass . . . and bits of broken glass . . . or fragments . . . pieces of glass . . . rubbish . . . (*Solemnly.*) Or else, if I'm nice, shards . . . splinters!

THE MOTHER, *who has entered, has been looking at and listening to her for a moment or two.*

THE MOTHER: You do things well.
LEILA: In my division, I'm unbeatable.
THE MOTHER (*pointing to* LEILA'*s bulging belly*): What's that?
LEILA (*laughing*): My latest little one.
THE MOTHER (*also laughing*): Got it where?
LEILA: In the house of Sidi Ben Cheik. I went in by the window. (*Smiling.*) Oh yes, I'm now able to climb through windows.
THE MOTHER: No one saw you? All right, put it there.

She points to a stool drawn on the screen in trompe-l'oeil. *With a charcoal pencil that she has taken from her pocket* LEILA *draws, above the table, a clock.* THE MOTHER *holds the candle while* LEILA *draws.*

THE MOTHER: You'll end by getting nabbed again. Especially since we can no longer hide anything, since because of you we no longer have a shack. We're reduced to the dump, the public dump, and it'll be easy to accuse us.

LEILA (*airily*): All right then, to the jug. With Saïd. Since we've now got to go from village to village, might as well go from jail to jail . . . with Saïd.

THE MOTHER: With? . . . With Saïd? . . . (*Threateningly.*) You're not stealing, I hope, so you can join Saïd?

LEILA (*with a very visible wink, visible despite her hood*): Why not?

THE MOTHER (*violently*): You wouldn't dare. And particularly since he doesn't want you.

LEILA: You know nothing about him since I've been with you.

THE MOTHER (*furiously*): For him, my son, you're just a poor device. (*She stands up and goes to strike* LEILA.)

LEILA (*airily*): Oh, don't worry, I'm not in love with him, with your darling virgin! (*A pause.*) I need something else.

THE MOTHER (*interested*): Oh! . . . Do you have something? Because you can't, after all, have some*one*. . . .

LEILA (*laughing*): Oh, not that! Neither anything, nor anyone, nor Saïd. (*Solemnly.*) I'm concerned with a great adventure.

THE MOTHER (*a little disconcerted*): What adventure?

LEILA (*mockingly*): Big mystery!

THE MOTHER: That of stinking more and more?

LEILA *laughs. She has finished the drawing of the clock, a magnificent one, Louis XV-style. At this moment,* LEILA *turns her back to* THE MOTHER, *who turns hers to the left wing.*

THE MOTHER (*moving the candle over the drawing*): It's pretty. What is it—real marble or imitation?

LEILA (*with pride*): Imitation.

Suddenly THE GENDARME *enters, left. He approaches very slowly and warily, taking long steps and looking about him without surprise.* LEILA *bows as she looks toward the right, that is, in the direction opposite that from which* THE GENDARME *is approaching.*

LEILA: I'm Saïd's wife. Come in, Mr. Gendarme.

THE GENDARME *looks about him again. He stares at the clock drawn on the screen.*

THE GENDARME: That's you all right. You were seen leaving the house of Sidi Ben Cheik. You pushed aside the beaded door-curtain. The beads rattled. . . . You were seen in a mirror, running away. . . . The clock was no longer there. (*A pause.*) Is that the one?

THE MOTHER: The clock's always been there. My husband brought it back from Lille.

THE GENDARME (*suspiciously*): How long ago?

THE MOTHER (*standing up*): Years ago. The clock's been there for ages. Just imagine, one day, when he was very little, Saïd took it completely apart. Completely. Piece by piece, to see what was inside, and he put all the springs on a plate. He was still a tot, and just then I entered the house. That was long ago, as you can imagine. I was returning from the grocer's, and what did I see on the floor? . . . (*She mimes the scene.*) But really, like some kind of vermin ready to scamper away: little wheels, little stars, little screws, little worms, little nails, gobs and gobs of thingumbobs, little springs, sparrows' wings, cigarettes, bayonets, castanets. . . .

During THE MOTHER's *spiel,* LEILA *sneaks toward the exit, but* THE GENDARME *turns around and catches her.*

LEILA: I was trying to run away.

THE GENDARME: To run away! . . . To fuck off! . . . To scram! . . . To hot-foot it! . . . And what does it get me? Dismissal. I gain my dismissal. Is that why you want to sneak away? So that I get shit from the sergeant, that's why! You little louse. And me, dope that I am, talking to you politely, like we're advised to do! They sure have funny notions, the boys up there at the top, with their politeness! I'd like to see them in close contact with you, like us little guys.

THE MOTHER: Little? You fellows aren't little to us.

THE GENDARME: Luckily we've got *you,* so that there are smaller ones than us, but if they make us call you "miss" and "madame," we'll soon be smaller than you.

THE MOTHER: From time to time you can forget the "miss" and "madame" and just call us "you there."

THE GENDARME: Because you prefer that, eh? "You there" is more intimate than "miss" and "madame," it protects you better than "miss" and "madame." Though "you there" protects you, you like "miss" and "madame" from time to time. I suppose you *do.*

THE MOTHER: A little "miss" and "madame," say one day out of four, and "you there" the rest of the time.

THE GENDARME: That's my view. "You there" as a basis, and "miss" and "madame" in droplets. To get used to it. We both gain by that. But if I suddenly say "madame," to whom do I say "you there"? Between me and you, "you there" is kind of palsy.

THE MOTHER: Right. "Madame" 's too-too. "You there" is woo-woo.

LEILA: "You there" 's taboo . . . "You there" pooh-pooh . . . Pooh-pooh on you . . . (*She laughs.* THE MOTHER *laughs.*)

THE MOTHER (*carrying on the game*): But who is who? . . . "You there" coo-coo . . . So toodle-oo. (*She laughs.* LEILA *laughs.* THE GENDARME *laughs.*)

THE GENDARME: So what's to do? . . . to do, to do, but pooh on . . . Who? . . . On who? . . . On "you there"! (*They all roar with laughter, but suddenly* THE GENDARME *realizes that he is sharing in the laughter. He explodes.*) Silence! What do you want? What are you trying to do? Fool me by laughing and pulling my leg? Lead me astray? (*The two women are frightened.*) I may be a little guy, O.K., but all the same I can't laugh, all the same I can't guffaw with the riff-raff. . . . (*He breathes deeply and calms down.*) It's enough we fraternize with your men talking about flags, about battles, talking about the Argonne, the Marne, you remember, Greaseball, it was you who carried the Tommy gun, I was the captain's orderly, the day we fired at the two Heinies, bang! Picked off by an Arab, that was what I call a battle royal and I'm not ashamed to remember it and still have a drink with the guy, not ashamed to. We don't mind feeling sentimental with your men, that's all right, from time to time, glad to. . . . (*A pause, then gravely.*) But laugh at the same time, no, that's overdoing it. I could tell you a thing or two about laughing, the laughing that doubles you up, the laughing that takes the edge off you. When you burst out laughing, everything opens up: mouth, nose, eyes, ears, asshole. Everything drains out of you, and who knows what fills in. (*Severely.*) You get me? Don't try to win me over with a bellylaugh. I can be ferocious. Haven't you seen how many molars I still have at the back of my mouth? (*He opens his mouth wide and the women seem frightened.*)

THE MOTHER: It happened just like that, suddenly, talking about "miss" and "madame" and "you there."

THE GENDARME: But it was you who *made* it happen. Let's not start again. Mustn't give you too much rope. Got to bring you round, little by little, without being thrown off. Neither you nor us, that's what I always say. But that can be done with the kind who understand and there *are* some, but with the kind that want to get us into trouble, we end up behind the eight ball. (*To* LEILA): And that one there, trying to sneak away! But if it's not me it's someone else who catches you and the result is we both get it in the neck, we're up the creek.

LEILA: That's what I deserve. That's what I want.

THE GENDARME: You'll get what's coming to you.

LEILA: Fine. I want to arrive in jail with my mug black and blue, my hair sticky with tears and snot, and my body all crooked because of a smashed rib. . . .

THE GENDARME: You know very well we can't treat you the way we used to. (*A little disconcerted.*) We want to be humane, I'm one of those who want to be humane, but it's you who look for trouble. About the clock, we'll discuss it up there with the sergeant. It's imitation marble, or real marble, you can bet it's imitation. The stuff that's sold in the villages and at fairs and markets nowadays! Nothing's like it used to be.

LEILA: The stuff you pick out of garbage cans is in more or less rotten condition.

THE GENDARME: That's sufficient grounds for punishment. Back home, it's bad enough to own a shoddy object, but to fill one's house with the stuff, that's beyond reason. Everything. We bring you everything—schools, hospitals, police stations, and to you it's all nothing. Hot air. Sand. A broken glass, a damaged clock. . . . (*He shrugs and turns to* LEILA.)

THE MOTHER: Take the blanket.

LEILA (*pointing to a blanket*): That one?

THE MOTHER: No, not that one. It hasn't enough holes.

THE GENDARME (*to* THE MOTHER): Giving her the one with the most holes?

THE MOTHER: What interests her is the holes. The more there are, the better she likes it. In fact, what she likes best is to wrap herself for the night in a big hole. The ideal thing would be for her to find one that only a north wind and the smell of manure pass through.

THE GENDARME: After all, make yourselves at home! . . . But if she really needed a hole made to order, my colleagues and I could get together and provide her with a fine one, so long by so wide, of such-and-such a shape. All in all, it would cost around so much. Don't worry about the hole, she'll have her hole, it's in the bag.

He leaves with LEILA. THE MOTHER *remains alone, for four seconds, then* THE GENDARME *re-enters, alone, ferocious-looking, dragging the blanket. At that moment, the clock drawn on the screen by* LEILA *lets out a very pleasant chime.* THE MOTHER *seems very proud of it.*

THE GENDARME: Moslem women! I know your tricks all right! One day—ah! Brittany, the fun you have there!—one carnival day with a sheet and a rag I disguised myself as an Arab woman, a Fatima. All at once, straight off, I grasped your mentality. Caught on in a flash. And if circumstances force me, in spite of my wound and my two daughters I'll take the veil again. (*Suiting his actions to his words, he rolls himself up in the blanket.*)

SCENE TEN

Three screens, five panels each, set up as follows: one rather near the footlights, center; the two others, which represent an orange grove, behind and on each side of the first. Each orange tree, with its oranges, is painted against a background of dark sky.

Two colonists: SIR HAROLD *and* MR. BLANKENSEE. *Three Arabs:* ABDIL, MALIK, NASSER.

Costumes:

SIR HAROLD *is in riding breeches.*

MR. BLANKENSEE: *Black and yellow striped trousers. Violet dress coat, wing collar—or stand-up collar—but very high.* MR. BLANKENSEE *is tall and strong. He has a big belly and a big behind (we shall soon know why). He has red sideburns and a red mustache.*
The three Arabs wear suits of European cut, but of bright and clashing colors.

SIR HAROLD *and* MR. BLANKENSEE *are watching the Arabs, who are standing in a row and hoeing the ground. Their gestures should give a strong impression of truth.*

SIR HAROLD (*grandiloquently*): Of Hainaut! . . . The Duchess of
Hainaut? . . . You say the Duchess of Hainaut? You were
talking about cork trees . . .

MR. BLANKENSEE (*proudly*): My roses first! They're my pride and
joy! My dear fellow, I think I have one of the finest rose
gardens in Africa . . . (*Upon* SIR HAROLD'*s making a gesture*):
. . . no, no, it's simply for my personal pleasure, my roses
are ruining me! My roses are my dancers. (*He laughs.*)
I mean it, in fact I get up at night to go and sniff them.

SIR HAROLD (*he looks at* ABDIL *and* MALIK, *who have stopped hoeing*):
At night? Can you find your way?

MR. BLANKENSEE (*smiling mischievously*): It's hard, of course, but
there's a trick to it. As I can't see them in the darkness
and yet want to be able to name them to myself and
caress them, I've attached to each rosebush a bell with a
different note. At night I can recognize them by their odor
and voice. My roses! (*Lyrically.*) With their strong, hard,
triangular thorns on stems as stern as guardsmen at
attention.

SIR HAROLD (*curtly*): And on windy nights you're in Switzerland
amidst a herd of cows. (*He continues in the same tone, now
speaking to* ABDIL): I've said that when you're here you're
to forget about your quarrels. An Arab's an Arab. You
should have attended to it earlier and got me another one.

MALIK: I know that an Arab's generally a good-for-nothing,
Sir Harold. But do you think it's nice to steal from a
fellow-worker's pocket? And for us to work with a thief?
To be bent over clods of earth at the same time as he, in
the same way as he, so that we don't know whether
thievery'll creep into our bodies by the same backache
as his?

SIR HAROLD: Did anyone warn me? Now that he's been taken

on, I'm keeping him.

A silence.

ABDIL: We were hoping to be able to get rid of him by ourselves.

SIR HAROLD (*incensed*): And why, pray? Am I no longer boss
here?

MALIK: Oh yes, of course you are, Sir Harold. You're our
father. Too bad we're not your children.

SIR HAROLD (*looking into the distance*): Where is he?

MALIK: He's pottering around with the lemon trees, by the
Nymph grove. The red you see there is the red of his
jacket.

SIR HAROLD (*furiously*): Ostracized! . . . You've ostracized him!
. . . Without orders from me, and without telling me! . . .

NASSER (*sharply*): If he takes a job, it's to be near the jackets
hanging from the branches or lying on the grass. All right.
But when it comes to work, he gums it up, he botches it,
he's a slob. And I'm not talking about his stink. When
he's within a yard of you, you feel all limp. The whole
crew is contaminated, dishonored. . . .

SIR HAROLD: Ostracized! And without orders from me! I want
him back. (*He yells.*) Saïd! (*To the others*): He's never
taken anything from *me*. And he'd better not try! So
whether he robs you or not, whether you like him or not,
he's an Arab like the others. He's working and he's on the
pay roll. He'll go clear the land with you. (*To* SAÏD, *who
must still be quite a way off*): You hear me? (*To the others*):
While you're working on the job, you're to cooperate. In
a line, one next to the other, moving forward with the
hoe, in the direction of the sun. That's clear. And no
quarreling. You're here on my land to work on it, and to
work in harmony. When you're at home, have all the

complications and—why not, you've a right to them—all the moral refinements you like. Is that clear too? All right, it'll be dark soon. Twilight's coming on. Go home. Good-by. (*The three Arabs, lined up with their hoes on their shoulders, leave, left. When they have disappeared, he cries out*): Abdil! . . . Nasser! . . . Saïd! . . . Malik! . . . tomorrow morning, on the job at four o'clock. While the ground's still damp. (*To* MR. BLANKENSEE): Not bad, eh? Must never forget to call them by their names: Abdil . . . Saïd . . . Malik . . . Nasser . . .

MR. BLANKENSEE (*to* SIR HAROLD): Quite the right tone. Both firm and familiar. Yet you've got to remain on guard. Because one day or other they may stand up to you . . . and answer back. . . .

SIR HAROLD: That's the danger. If they get into the habit of answering, they'll get into the habit of thinking as well. And yet! . . . I use three hundred fifty of them. I can no longer lead them with a whip. I've got to be careful. (*He looks about him.*) That Saïd . . . He's quite a card! Like the others, after all, neither worse . . .

As SIR HAROLD *and* MR. BLANKENSEE *make the following speeches, they walk up and down, turning their backs slightly to the screens. Darkness comes on gradually.*

MR. BLANKENSEE: You're armed, of course. (SIR HAROLD *slaps his holster.*) What about your European foremen?

SIR HAROLD: All of them. But there are times I distrust them. You know them: Italians, Spaniards, Maltese . . . and even a Greek from Corfu . . . and communism in the air.

While they speak, an Arab enters, bending forward. At the foot of each orange tree, he draws a yellow flame with chalk, then disappears.

MR. BLANKENSEE: I import all mine from the shores of the Rhine. Discipline . . . honesty . . . it's the laborers that worry me.

SIR HAROLD: You're . . .?

MR. BLANKENSEE (*snapping to attention*): Dutch. My great-great-grandpa. But it's more recent on my wife's side. Her father was an official. Post Office Department. (*A pause.*) One can rightly say that it's men like us who made this country.

SIR HAROLD: You grow cork oaks?

MR. BLANKENSEE: One-hundred-five thousand one-hundred-twelve trunks! (SIR HAROLD *makes a gesture of admiration.*) Can't complain, except I now have to reckon with Portugal, whose prices are very low. Plus the fact that plastic corks are being used more and more. It's true they last longer, but they don't give wine and mineral water the bouquet that the cork from these parts does. Had to close my corkscrew factory—it was inevitable. A gleam of hope! when with the monstrous increase of noise back home they thought of lining walls with cork boards. A short-lived hope, unfortunately. Intensified fight against noise and use of new techniques—artificial, like all the rest—of soundproofing.

SIR HAROLD: What new techniques?

MR. BLANKENSEE: Compressed cork powder.

Another Arab has entered and, in the same way as the first, draws flames at the foot of the orange trees of the second screen.

SIR HAROLD: That saves you!

MR. BLANKENSEE (*with disgust*): They mix it with sawdust. And what sawdust! Scandinavian larchwood! Everything is doctored. But the essential thing is that my rose garden be saved. Much has been said, and will be said, against the colonizers, but it's thanks to one of the most modest

of them that there's such a fine rose garden here! . . .
(*He recovers his breath a little and, smiling, opens his trouser
belt a few notches, explaining*): That's my pad. . . . . (*Then
he shows his whole orthopedic outfit.*)

SIR HAROLD (*interested*): Ah ha, you wear a pad. On your
backside too, no doubt.

MR. BLANKENSEE: To balance the other. A man of my age who
doesn't have a belly and ass hasn't much prestige. So one
has to fake a little. . . . (*A slight silence.*) In the old days,
there were wigs. . . . It's well adjusted. (*He shows it again.*)

SIR HAROLD: But the chambermaid . . .

MR. BLANKENSEE: Oh, doesn't know about it. I'm discreet. It's
as delicate a matter as dentures or a glass eye in a glass
of water. Personal secrets. (*A sigh.*) Yes, it takes all that
faking to impose ourselves . . . to be imposing! But I've
come to see you to ask your help in working out a defense
plan. . . .

SIR HAROLD: As I was saying before, one of the ringleaders,
Slimane, has been killed. The whole region's beginning
to effervesce. (*Offering his cigarette case*): Cigarette? . . .
A light? . . . (*A third Arab has entered, like the first two, and
draws flames at the foot of the third screen.*) You know that,
despite the watchfulness of the rural police, ten or twenty
telegraph poles are cut down every night. Trees already
killed, that's true, but next they'll go after the olive trees
. . . millenial trees, that's also true, but then it'll be the
orange trees, the . . .

MR. BLANKENSEE (*carrying on*): . . . cork oaks. I love my cork
oaks. There's nothing more beautiful than a forest of cork
oaks when the men circle round the trunk to strip it of
its bark. And when the flesh of the tree appears, raw and
bleeding! People may laugh at us, at our love of this
country, but you (*He is moved.*), you know that our love is
real. It's we who made it, not they! Try to find a single

one of them who can talk about it as we do! And about the thorns of my roses.

SIR HAROLD: Say a word or two about them.

MR. BLANKENSEE (*as if he were reciting Mallarmé*): The stem, straight and stiff. The green foliage, sound and glazed, and on the stem and in the foliage, the thorns. You can't joke with the rose as you can with the dahlia. The thorns mean that this flower's not to be trifled with, all those sentinels watching over it, strongholds if you like, warriors! —they exact respect even from a chief of state. We're the lords of language. To tamper with roses is to tamper with language.

SIR HAROLD *applauds delicately.*

SIR HAROLD: And to tamper with language is sacrilegious.

An Arab comes crawling in. He blows on the fire drawn at the foot of the orange trees. The gentlemen do not see him.

MR. BLANKENSEE: In a German operetta, I forget which, a character says: "Things belong to those who've known how to improve them . . ." Who is it who's improved your orange groves, and my forests and roses? My rose bushes are my blood. There was a moment when I thought the troops . . .

A second Arab crawls in. Like the first, he stirs up the fire.

SIR HAROLD: Naïveté. The army's playing with itself, like a lad behind a fence. It prefers itself to all else . . . (*Bitterly.*) . . . and particularly to your roses.

MR. BLANKENSEE: Think we ought to clear out?

SIR HAROLD (*proudly*): I have a son. And to save my son's

patrimony, I'd sacrifice my son.

MR. BLANKENSEE (*same tone*): To save my roses . . . (*Vexed.*)
. . . I have no one to sacrifice.

*A third Arab crawls in. He, too, blows on the fire drawn at the foot
of the orange trees, he stirs it with his hand.* SIR HAROLD *and*
MR. BLANKENSEE *leave, right. Then, from behind the screens five or
six more Arabs, dressed like the others, come crawling in. They draw
flames and blow on them.* SAÏD *is not among them. A loud crackling of
burning trees (the sound is made in the wings).* SIR HAROLD *and* MR.
BLANKENSEE *reappear, left. They seem very animated by their discussion and do not see the cataclysm. The Arabs immediately disappear
behind the screen.*

SIR HAROLD (*playing with his switch*): And besides, even if we
wanted to, how could *we* make the subtle distinction
between an Arab who's a thief and an Arab who's not?
How do they themselves manage it? If a Frenchman robs
me, that Frenchman's a thief, but if an Arab robs me,
he hasn't changed. He's an Arab who has robbed me, and
nothing more. Isn't that the way you see it? (*More and
more loudly and animatedly.*) There's no proprietorship in
immorality—pornographic writers are aware of the fact.
They can never complain before a court that another
pornographer has robbed them of a . . . a disgusting
situation. (MR. BLANKENSEE *laughs heartily.*) No proprietorship in immorality, that's the formula. (*More and more
loudly, sniffing.*) Smells of jam! I don't mean, mind you,
that they have no code of ethics. What I say is that in
no case can their ethics be modeled on ours. (*Suddenly
uneasy.*) And they probably suspect as much. Although,
just before, our three lascars—a word we pinched from
them, by the way, a word of theirs but one we quickly
brought into line—although our three lascars recognized

the fact that one of their fellows is a thief, they hesitated a long time before telling me. . . . Oh, oh! . . . it's because there's something in the air. . . . And that Saïd, whose reputation keeps swelling! I ought to have . . .

They leave again, going behind the screens. Ten or twelve Arabs, dressed like the others, crawl in. They blow on the flames and draw them so big that all the orange trees are aglow. By the time SIR HAROLD *and* MR. BLANKENSEE *re-enter, right, the Arabs have disappeared.*

Both men seem very excited by their discussion.

MR. BLANKENSEE: . . . of a well-thought-out policy. But the Army doesn't want to get mixed up in it. It seeks out the enemy the way a dog seeks out game. The Army doesn't give a damn that my roses and your oranges are in danger. If need be, it would sack everything to have a wilder time . . .

SIR HAROLD (*as if preoccupied*): I ought to have . . .

MR. BLANKENSEE: What, my dear fellow?

SIR HAROLD: . . . suspected it. (*A pause.*) For some time they'd stopped believing in the watchful virtues of my pigskin glove. (*Even more anxiously.*) Furthermore, my glove itself no longer kept me informed.

MR. BLANKENSEE: Those jerks'll end by making us intelligent.

SCENE ELEVEN

In the foreground, that is, on the floor of the stage, two screens: three panels at the right, three at the left. At the foot of each of the screens, which represent the prison, is a black stool chained to the screen. SAÏD is stretched out at the foot of the right screen. LEILA is squatting at the left. In the center of the stage, a chair, in which THE GUARD is sitting and snoring. A third screen will enter presently, right, on a rather high platform set back from the aforementioned screens. It will represent Mr. and Mrs. Blankensee's window and balcony. But before it enters, a sky-blue screen will appear, left, on an even higher platform, which is set back from the other. It is in front of this screen that THE LIEUTENANT and members of the Foreign Legion will accouter themselves.

LEILA (*in a very gentle voice*): . . . if you had walked fast, and bent forward, and especially if your jacket had been unbuttoned, nobody would have noticed the canned goods bulging under your shirt.

SAÏD (*same tone*): If you're right, you idiot, it's even worse, since you're showing me how to escape now that it's too late. You should have told me before. . . .

LEILA: I was already in jail. Locked up in the jug. I couldn't advise you. . . .

SAÏD: I don't want advice, but you can guide me, since you're invisible and far away, behind walls . . . walls that are thick . . . and white. . . . (*A pause.*) You, where do *you* stink most?

LEILA (*in ecstasy*): Oh me! *Who* isn't thunderstruck at my approach? When I arrive, the night falls back. . . .

SAÏD (*in ecstasy*): In confusion?

A VOICE (*very loudly, off-stage*): As soon as the hosts and the Latin have been swallowed. . . .

Suddenly, a kind of bugle call, imitated by a mouth. It is then that the screen slides in on the high platform. We see, in silhouette, five Legionnaires, kneeling. They stand up. THE LIEUTENANT, who has just entered, bareheaded, puts on his képi. As he speaks the screen becomes opaque again.

THE LIEUTENANT (*it is he who was speaking*): . . . have coffee served, piping hot. You, the stretcher bearers, take apart the portable altar, and you, Mr. Chaplain, crucifix, surplice, chalices and ciboria, in the kit. (THE LIEUTENANT *puts on his crossbelt.*) My gloves! (*A Legionnaire comes out from behind the screen and hands him a pair of gray leather gloves.*) White ones. (*The soldier disappears for a second, reappears with a pair of white gloves, salutes and leaves. THE LIEUTENANT continues, putting on his gloves very carefully.*) Rarin' to go. Rarin' . . . and tough, dammit! Your beds of love are the battlefield. . . . In war as in love! Arrayed for battle! In full array, gentlemen. (*He stares at the audience.*) . . . I want the Army to send your families wristwatches and medals caked with blood and even with jissom. I want . . . Preston! . . . my revolver . . . I want the peaks of your képis to be shinier than my boots, more highly polished than my nails. . . . (*Enter* PRESTON, *another Legionnaire, who hands the officer the holster containing the revolver, and then leaves.* THE

LIEUTENANT *hooks it to his belt while speaking.*) . . . your buttons, buckles, clips, hooks, like my spurs: chrome-plated . . . Warfare, screwing . . . I want pictures of naked babes and holy virgins sewn into your linings. Around your necks, gold chains, or gold-plated . . . On your hair, brilliantine, ribbons in the hair on your ass—for those who have hair, but God damn it, a soldier should be hairy!—and handsome. . . . Preston! . . . my field glasses. (*Same business as above:* PRESTON *brings the field glasses in their case.* THE LIEUTENANT *carefully puts the strap around his neck, then opens the case and surveys the landscape. Then, he puts the glasses back into the case, and . . . in short, he is acting.*) Hairy . . . and handsome! Don't forget. Good warriors, brave warriors, of course, but above all handsome warriors. Therefore: perfect soldiers, rectified by artifice if necessary. Muscular necks. Work on your necks . . . by torsion, tension, contraction, distortion, suspension, compression, flexion, fluction. . . . Hard thick thighs. Or seemingly so. Knee-high, beneath your underpants . . . Preston! my boots! (*Enter* PRESTON, *who kneels in front of the officer and rubs his boots with a rag.*) . . . beneath your underpants, put sandbags to swell your knees, but look like gods! Your gun . . .

A VOICE: B'jesus, b'jesus! Sandbags in the gods' pants! Upholstered gods! Did you hear that, boys?

THE SERGEANT *appears and salutes* THE LIEUTENANT. *His fatigue-jacket is unbuttoned, and he doesn't care. His fly, too, is half open.*

THE LIEUTENANT (*continuing*): Your gun, waxed, polished, scrubbed, supreme adornment its bayonet, crown jewel, lily of the oriflamme, the bayonet, its steel more pitiless than the eye of the Sergeant. . . .

THE SERGEANT (*at attention*): Here, sir.

THE LIEUTENANT: At ease. And your eye like the bayonet. And screwing. Get me: war's a rip-roaring orgy. Triumphant awakening! Make my boots shine! You're the mighty prick of France who dreams she's fucking! My boots more brilliant, Preston! I want war and screwing in the sun! And guts oozing in the sun! Get it?

THE SERGEANT: Got it.

THE LIEUTENANT: Right?

A VOICE (*behind the screens*): Right.

THE LIEUTENANT: We'll approach under cover of darkness, but it's at dawn, when the sun blazes forth, that we'll enter. There'll be blood . . . yours or that of the others. It doesn't matter. You'll be sensitive to the liquid, wherever it flows from. . . . You, Walter?

The following speeches are to be spoken at top speed.

VOICE OF WALTER (*behind the screen*): Both my hands cut off, both my feet cut off, and if my blood spurts in four jets that fall back into my open mug . . .

During this time is heard the light snoring of LEILA, SAÏD *and* THE GUARD.

THE LIEUTENANT: Fine. You, Hernandez?

VOICE OF HERNANDEZ: No. The blood'll spring not from *my* guts but from the one I gut!

THE LIEUTENANT: You, Brandineschi?

VOICE OF BRANDINESCHI: Blood, Sir. Mine. Yours. That of the others or that of the stones, but blood.

After saying his lines, each soldier sits down in an attitude of boredom.

THE LIEUTENANT: Ready?

At this moment, enter, right, the screen representing the window of the Blankensee house. .

A VOICE: Ready.

THE LIEUTENANT: Foul language? So long as we remain in a faraway land, let the hills echo with your wildest oaths. (*To* THE SERGEANT): Sergeant! Your men are brushing up their Foreign Legion oaths, I hope? I want the men to be: lyrical, realistic, horny. (*He is suddenly calmer, almost gentle.*) But gentlemen, behind those hills it's men you'll have to gut, not rats. But the Arabs are rats. For a split second, in the hand-to-hand fighting, take a good look at them —if they give you time—and discover, but fast, the humanity that's in them. Otherwise, you'd be killing rats, and you'd have waged war and made love only with rats. (*He looks very sad, almost discouraged.*) Get it?

THE SERGEANT (*He takes out a package of cigarettes. He drops one.* THE LIEUTENANT *picks it up and hands it to him. Without a word* THE SERGEANT *puts it into his mouth*): Got it.

THE LIEUTENANT (*same tone of discouragement*): Right? (*While* PRESTON *shines his boots,* THE LIEUTENANT *examines the auditorium with his field glasses.*

THE SERGEANT (*calmly buttoning his trousers and fatigue jacket*): Right.

LEILA (*waking up*): It's up to you to be careful. And crafty.

SAÏD (*also waking up*): But it's up to you to show me the way of escape before God cuts it off. You're of no use to me.

LEILA (*ironically*): Get it?

SAÏD: Got it.

LEILA (*same tone*): Right?

SAÏD: Right.

LEILA: Except to your shame. And yet you take for granted that I do what has to be done in order to join you in jail.

SAÏD (*very annoyed*): I take for granted that shame, like shadow,

walks and gleams beside or behind me. (*A pause.*) Tell me
why you took the side paths instead of going by the
highway. By the highway no one would have seen or
noticed you. By the side paths they smelled your theft,
since you reek of theft.

LEILA: You're always right, afterwards. It was after I was ugly
that you married me. (*A pause.*) But tell me why you
didn't take money from the grocer's till. She'd sold all
her soap. . . .

SAÏD: When I went by again, two hours later, her grandfather
was in the store. He was counting the packages of tapioca.
I had to help him.

LEILA (*with excessive pity*): But, poor Saïd, you don't know how
to count.

SAÏD: I can't read or write, but count I can.

A pause.

LEILA: Though I'm shrewish and mean . . . (*A pause.*) Saïd . . .

SAÏD: Shit.

LEILA (*softly*): Saïd . . . I'm now good at begging.

SAÏD (*admiringly*): Panhandling? And you only tell me that
tonight?

THE GUARD (*awake and standing; in a gruff, vulgar tone*): . . . What
with always yelling and screaming at you, because of you
I have godawful nights. Let the night get some rest. The
night needs silence too. From one end of Moslem soil to
the other there's nothing but muttering in the shadow,
cracking of branches, cigarette lighters sputtering, olive
trees blazing, prowlers who leave behind a smell of
burning, rebellions . . . and you two, you two, in your
rags . . . you never . . . stop . . . singing. . . . (*He dozes off.*)

SAÏD (*continuing a conversation with* LEILA): It's dark in my cell
too. The only light I get comes from your decayed teeth,

your dirty eyes, your dull skin. Your lazy eyes, your hazy eyes, one looking off to Rio de Janeiro and the other staring into the bottom of a cup: that's you. And your dull skin, an old silk muffler around the neck of a public-school teacher: that's you.

LEILA: Yet I willingly went down where you told me and it wasn't to the bottom of a cup of milk! I now go there all by myself. And I even have to be almost held back by the skirt. . . .

SAÏD: Are there still any places in you that could be bowed to? If you see any . . .

LEILA: There must be, but the one who bows to them—boyohboy!—has to have a strong stomach. . . . (*A pause.*) You've never beaten me, Saïd.

SAÏD: I spend all my nights training. As soon as I get out, you'll get it in the puss.

A silence. A voice is heard.

THE VOICE (*very manly and decided*): No. If it were to do over again, I wouldn't come up from behind with a sickle this time. I'd approach from the front, smiling, and I'd offer her an artificial flower, the kind she liked. A violet satin iris. She'd thank me. No blonde doll, like those in the movies, would have listened to the kind of drivel I dished out, and with a winning smile. It was only . . .

LEILA (*admiringly*): Who's that?

THE GUARD (*grumblingly*): The condemned man. He killed his mother.

THE VOICE: . . . when my speech was finished and she had smelled the rose and stuck it in her gray hair that I'd have (THE VOICE *gradually becomes exultant; toward the end, it intones and sings.*) . . . delicately opened her belly, I'd have lifted up the curtains of the skirt to watch the guts flow

and I'd have toyed with them as fingers toy with jewels.
And my eyes' joy would have sparkled in the haunted
eyes of my mother.

A silence.

SAÏD (*sadly*): He's reached the point where he can sing.
THE GUARD (*roughly*): Where he *must* sing. And you beginners,
shut up!

*A silence. We hear a few bars of the "Marseillaise" played on a
harmonica.* LEILA *and* SAÏD *shut their eyes.* THE GUARD *is snoring.
The light goes on. We are in the Blankensees' bedroom.* MRS.
BLANKENSEE *is in front of the window drawn on the screen. She is
holding a revolver which is pointed in front of her.* MR. BLANKENSEE
is looking for something in the room. MRS. BLANKENSEE *is wearing a
mauve negligee.*

MR. BLANKENSEE: But where . . .
MRS. BLANKENSEE (*interrupting him*): Put out the light.

The light goes out. They talk in semi-darkness.

MRS. BLANKENSEE (*in a whisper*): F sharp. (*She imitates the tinkle
of a bell.*)
MR. BLANKENSEE (*also in a whisper*): Someone's touched Madame
Foch.
MRS. BLANKENSEE: Where is she?
MR. BLANKENSEE: Near the entrance, under the gum tree . . .
(*A pause.*) Don't be afraid, dear. The rose garden's full of
traps. I myself have set man traps on all the paths. (*He
grinds his teeth.*) Like your teeth—don't you feel how the
steel jaws simply can't wait any more? They're going to
have to bite.

MRS. BLANKENSEE (*thrilled*): You're here. (*A pause.*) Did you have the impression this morning that something's stirring in the Arab town?

MR. BLANKENSEE: Everything's stirring. The calm is so intense it's as if everything were stirring at tremendous speed.

MRS. BLANKENSEE: They want to impress us . . .

MR. BLANKENSEE: Or else they're afraid . . .

MRS. BLANKENSEE: It comes to the same. . . . (*A gesture.*) Something's moving. . . .

MR. BLANKENSEE: It's the cypress. I'll go and see. . . . I'd like to know whether one's been caught. Whether he's clenching his teeth not to scream, and why every steel jaw isn't screaming. . . . (*He seems to be looking for something.*) Where is . . .

MRS. BLANKENSEE: What? Your pad? . . . The maid discovered it this morning while doing the room. She took it to mend.

MR. BLANKENSEE (*staggered*): Discovered it! . . . Took it! . . . To mend! . . .

MRS. BLANKENSEE: You shouldn't have forgotten it. It's your own fault. You've been forgetting to wear it the last few days and been letting it lie around. . . . You're getting careless, and it's the wrong time. . . .

MR. BLANKENSEE: And . . . you think she suspects? . . .

MRS. BLANKENSEE: They're getting sharp-witted. . . . Are you going outside?

MR. BLANKENSEE: Among my roses? Without my pad on my belly? What would I look like? My pad is the chief element of my glamour. So are my boots. What perfume would my roses have without my boots to make me smell them?

MRS. BLANKENSEE (*sympathetically*): I know, darling. It's like me without my false hair, but since it's dark. . . . (*Artfully.*) Go to your roses the way you come to me, in your underpants. . . .

MR. BLANKENSEE (*excited, and embracing her*): The enemy is all about us. I no longer have a pad . . . neither on my ass nor on my belly. . . . Everything's betraying us, but you, you're here. . . .

MRS. BLANKENSEE: My love! Betrayal's not what it used to be. In the old days, as my great-grandmother used to tell me, an engaged couple would marry on the eve of their wedding. The male would gash the female, and an invisible red spot under her white gown would prove that love was stronger than God. One had to believe in God, of course, and betray. When the morning of the sacrament arrived, the wreath of orange blossom was very lovely!

THE GUARD (*asleep*): A whole life on sin!

MRS. BLANKENSEE: A whole life of love built on sin, as my great-grandmother explained to me. Love's beginning with an act of betrayal was perpetuated like the secret wound of an order one still respects.

MR. BLANKENSEE: And so you think it's because of that?

A bell tinkles.

MRS. BLANKENSEE (*panicky*): Be quiet! . . . They're there! . . .

MR. BLANKENSEE (*implacably*): You think it's because I married you intact and led you to the altar intact that everything's blowing up? . . .

MRS. BLANKENSEE (*as in orgasm*): My beloved, everything's blowing up! . . .

We very clearly see MRS. BLANKENSEE, *deeply moved, fire the pistol. Darkness at this screen.*

LEILA (*in a gutteral tone, and talking like a pitchman trying to gather a crowd at a fair*): Who . . . who? . . . And who still hasn't seen Saïd flipping and flopping when the cops get to work on him! And drooling blood and bleeding snot and oozing from every hole . . . who hasn't seen? . . .

SAÏD (*same tone*): And my wife, who hasn't seen her running away? Go see her, go see her!—running from under the stones, and when they fling bags of guess what, and from under the pommeling . . .

Each tries to scream more loudly than the other.

LEILA: . . . my man around the jackets . . .

SAÏD: . . . She runs head down, her hands and legs writhing . . .

LEILA: . . . prowling, crawling on all fours in the grass, his belly scraping up everything . . .

SAÏD: The woman the birds in the sky shitting on her so you become a stone statue. Magnificent in the daylight . . .

LEILA: . . . so cautious, so brisk, so green that he's a patch of leeks, so gray that he's my dry skin . . .

SAÏD: . . . that the day instead of coming on went away so as to let her triumph in her glory! (*We hear the sound of machine-gun fire in the distance.*) One sure thing, it's nice and sheltered here for squabbling with Leila. (*He is interrupted by* THE VOICE.)

THE VOICE: Madame, it's for my freedom's sake. Madame, I love only your belly, where for nine months I took the pink shape that the pink of your womb dropped on the floor like a fishball on a plate. Today I free myself for good from your overheated belly! I chill it. At twilight, tomorrow, when the first star comes up, I'm to be hanged, but the one who'll be hanged has the nimbleness of the gazelle, its invisibility. (*He intones.*) I have known war and in war sacred defeat! Fire! And sword! Light has need of shade!

SAÏD: A beggarwoman . . .

LEILA: . . . stinks. That's her stock in trade. You give her a penny and run away puking.

A brief silence.

SAÏD (*admiringly*): You're going to panhandle!

A longer silence.

THE GUARD (*half-awaking*): You at it again? Night is meant for sleeping. Be quiet, lovebirds, and sleep.

While LEILA *and* SAÏD *were talking, the Legionnaires, who had stood up silently as* MR. BLANKENSEE *was saying, above: "The calm is so intense," were busying themselves: closing knapsacks, arranging their cartridge belts, etc. Suddenly, as earlier, a mouth imitates the blare of a bugle. They all stand at attention. They salute a flag which is in the right wing, then, describing a curve, go behind the screen. They walk with heavy steps, as if setting out on a long journey.* THE SERGEANT, *who has not finished buttoning himself, remains alone.* THE GUARD *of the prison squirms in his chair.* SAÏD *and* LEILA *seem to be asleep.*

THE GUARD (*giving a military salute as the bugle call ceases*): Here, sir! (*Then he seems to wake up, and, facing upstage, cries out.*) That you again playing the kazoo? Tomorrow morning, before dawn, you'll be in the guardhouse. (*He yawns, sits down again and seems to doze off, then imitates to himself the speeches above.*) Get it? . . . Got it. Right? . . . Right.

He falls asleep. THE SERGEANT *is standing in front of the upper screen. He finally buttons his fly, then his fatigue jacket.* THE LIEUTENANT *approaches him and looks at him for a moment in silence.*

THE LIEUTENANT: In a little while we'll be within an ace of

death. . . . We're in for close fighting . . . they're waiting
for us behind the casbah. . . .

THE SERGEANT (*in a limp tone*): I'm ready.

THE LIEUTENANT (*staring at* THE SERGEANT): I don't doubt it.
You have the transparent eyes of tall, red-haired Scotch-
men. The Saxon eye, icier than the Germanic. And so
sad at times . . .

THE SERGEANT: Do you often look at my eyes?

THE LIEUTENANT: I'm a leader and do my job properly. I
observe them. . . . When your peak's not down too far.
(*With his own handkerchief he wipes* THE SERGEANT'*s cross belt.*
THE SERGEANT *does not stir.*)

THE SERGEANT (*continuing to button up*): What I'd like is to weave
me a crown of cornflowers and periwinkles! . . . To sit
by the river sewing on my buttons . . . To snuggle all
naked into white sheets . . . (*A pause.*) A big girl who's
just hung out her washing, and running . . .

THE LIEUTENANT (*sternly*): You're icy-eyed; you're a born
warrior.

THE SERGEANT (*he picks up his pack and loads it*): . . . A big girl
running, behold, it's really true I can't catch up with her,
she runs so fast on her heels . . .

THE LIEUTENANT: In a little while we'll be within an ace of
death. So will she, the girl who's just hung out her
washing. Afterwards, she'll have had her day, as the saying
goes. Her gait will be a little heavier. You'll see her
breathing under her dress. Perhaps you'll be united. Are
you ready? . . . They're attacking with grenades. . . .
We'll try to block them between the casbah and the
cemetery. You're a born warrior. The proof is that the
peak of your képi is always a little too far down over your
eyes . . . which it veils.

SCENE TWELVE

The screen (six panels) represents a kind of long, high, white crenelated rampart. (One might do better to use three screens, one behind and two in front on either side.) Ten or twelve Arabs in either European or Oriental dress (multicolored). Brilliant light—full floodlights—on the rampart and the crowd.

THE DIGNITARY (*wearing a fez and a blue, western-style suit with many decorations. Into the wings*): Remain quiet. Everyone must be dignified. No children here. Nor women.

KADIDJA (*the old woman who prevented* THE MOTHER *from mourning*): Without women what would you be? A spot of sperm on your father's pants that three flies would have drunk up.

THE DIGNITARY: Go away, Kadidja. This isn't the day.

KADIDJA (*furiously*): It is! They accuse us and threaten us, and you want us to be prudent. And docile. And humble. And submissive. And ladylike. And honey-tongued. And sweet as pie. And silk veil. And fine cigarette. And nice kiss and soft-spoken. And gentle dust on their red pumps!

THE DIGNITARY: Kadidja, it's a matter of general security. Go away.

KADIDJA: I won't! (*She stamps her heel.*) This is *my* town here.

My bed is here. I was fucked fourteen times here and gave birth to fourteen Arabs. I won't go.

THE DIGNITARY: See to it that she leaves or that she's gagged!

A Chief has already come up silently. Veiled and wearing silk and gold cloth, he bows before the crenelated screen. KADIDJA *is about to be taken away, but the first measures of the "Marseillaise" are struck up.* KADIDJA *tries to scream, facing the audience, but a man puts his fist into her mouth. She keeps it there until the end of the scene that follows. The Arabs remain motionless. A silence. Clusters of French flags rise to the tops of the screens. Continued silence. Then, at the tops of the screens, visible from the waist up, appear:* THE ACADEMICIAN; THE SOLDIER; THE VAMP, *with her cigarette holder; a news* PHOTOGRAPHER; *a widow* (MRS. BLANKENSEE); THE JUDGE; THE BANKER; THE LITTLE GIRL, *wearing a communion dress; and* THE GENERAL. *They are all in costumes of the 1840's:* THE SOLDIER *in uniform of the period,* THE VAMP *with lace umbrella,* THE BANKER *with sideburns and top hat, etc. They are all resting their elbows as on a parapet or looking off into space. They speak among themselves. The Arabs are silent. The following speeches are uttered at very great speed.*

THE PHOTOGRAPHER (*to* THE VAMP): In evening gown, on the ramparts, you'll be marvelous!

THE VAMP *elegantly throws back her fur piece and, at the same time, exhales a mouthful of smoke. Yes, the 1840* VAMP *may smoke, it doesn't matter.*

THE VAMP (*laughing*): Do you think it's hot there in the desert? I shiver there. But not with fear, don't worry about that! (*She laughs.*) Is heat really hot? Who can tell?

THE ACADEMICIAN: Place your pretty finger on the book of History. It burns there, for the word France is written

in letters of fire . . . or letters of ice, which also burns . . .
or letters of sulphuric acid, which likewise burns. . . .

THE VAMP (*laughing*): But where are your savages? One
doesn't see much of the rebellion. The uprisings . . .

THE SOLDIER: In my pants, Mademoiselle . . .

THE ACADEMICIAN (*interrupting him*): Roman. If not for you
no roads. And if no roads, no postmen. And if no postmen,
no post cards. (*A pause.*) And they continue to take side
paths! . . .

THE PHOTOGRAPHER: . . . only the beating of the Bedouin
drums!

THE ACADEMICIAN (*to* THE SOLDIER): Roman. You are the
Romans of this epic. (*To* THE VAMP): They are the Romans
of our time, and yet History never repeats itself. My dear
General . . .

THE GENERAL: We're doing what we can to win adherents.
The masses are friendly to us. One of them, in any case.
The other mass is hostile and we have to keep watch on
two fronts.

THE ACADEMICIAN: Trust and mistrust are the twin founts of
victory. (*To* THE SOLDIER): Isn't that so, young man?

THE SOLDIER: I know only my chief. . . . (*A silence.*) I don't
go for fine talk. (*A silence.*) . . . but my chief's my chief
and I respect him. . . .

THE VAMP: Why do they sometimes write . . . "a muttering of
rebellion . . ."? It's silent. . . .

THE SOLDIER (*forcefully*): The fact remains that manly beauty
means *us*. I've read it. The desert would be limp and
flabby without the rebel and without the soldier. Is there
anyone who can pull off our weather-beaten masks?
Goddamn it! All the effort one makes to be primed for
action for its own sake, aimed at victory if necessary
and death if you like, and to think there are masks still
not weather-beaten! . . (*A pause.*) There's flabbiness,
no question about it, there's still flabby flesh around . . . .

(*A pause, then, with decision.*) Got to be bone!

THE VAMP (*applauding*): Bravo for bone.

THE BANKER: The desert's not only big, it's thick.

THE ACADEMICIAN: Desert! The word has a certain ring!

THE GENERAL (*with outstretched arm*): To bear our conquests, our fame, ever southward. And our Sahara territories even farther south: some day they'll be our land of plenty.

THE ACADEMICIAN: With a cathedral pointing skyward. Its stained glass gleaming. And pilgrimages of young Moslems reading Péguy in the original. (*His eye suddenly lights up.*) Ah, General, the teen-age Moslem! (*He smacks his tongue knowingly.*)

THE SOLDIER (*looking* THE GENERAL *in the eyes*): Beware. One starts by taking a shine to the teen-age Moslem. Three months later one understands him. Then, one pleads his cause. And in the end, one's a traitor to the race. (*A pause.*) That's how it all began.

Embarrassed silence. Then, a slight hubbub. They all put their heads together, whisper, and burst out laughing.

THE PHOTOGRAPHER: Sen-sa-tion-al! A sensational shot! The flies! The famous oriental flies, huge, tremendous. Around the corpse and even at the corner of the kid's eyes. The photo was buzzing!

THE VAMP: You're going to make me vomit.

THE BANKER: Don't be shy, my dear, puke to your heart's content. It won't be lost on everyone.

General laughter.

THE SOLDIER: Our boys are buried everywhere. In the sand,

the weather-beaten masks, eyes looking one way and mouth the other. In the sand!

THE GENERAL: Each of us must assume his responsibilities. The Army will do its duty. The communiqués are excellent. Drafted in flawless French: terse, firm, sound, reassuring . . .

THE BANKER: . . . informative.

A silence.

THE LITTLE GIRL: I, too, have a word to say. I've kept a piece of holy bread in my alms purse. I want to crumble it for the birds of the desert, the poor darlings.

Suddenly a shot rings out from somewhere. THE LITTLE GIRL *falls backwards. The characters at the top of the screen (or of the three screens) look at each other in consternation, then disappear. Below,* THE ARAB *removes his fist from* KADIDJA's *mouth.* THE CHIEF *goes off, bent double. The Arabs leave with a frightened look, except* KADIDJA. *Thus, the stage is empty. Darkness. A rather long pause. Above, on a platform, appears a second screen, all gilded. On this platform stands a very tall dummy (eight or nine feet), center of the stage. It is covered from top to bottom with all kinds of decorations. Near it, a field glass, mounted on a tripod. A woman is perched on a chair and pinning a decoration on the dummy's shoulder. Near the chair stands an old gentleman—in morning jacket and striped trousers —bearing on his palms a cushion to which are pinned thirty or forty different kinds of medals.*

THE MAN: What about the ears?

THE WOMAN: (*curtly*): Once and for all, one doesn't pin decorations on the ears. On the behind . . . the sleeves . . . the thighs . . . the belly. . . . Hand me the blue one . . . no, the sky-blue one.

THE MAN: Grand Ribbon of the Holy Lamb!

THE WOMAN: (*pinning*): Why not? It's ours. Long reserved for plenipotentiaries. . . . There aren't so many left that you can spit on it. Let me have the star, I'll stick it on the inner side of the left thigh.

THE MAN: The spot where he might have been hit by a bullet.

THE WOMAN (*contemptuously*): A bullet! If only he could be hit by even a club there'd still be hope. Let me have the Cross of the Northern Splendor and the Holy Name. I'll pin it above the Academic Laurels. (*Which she does. Then, stepping off the chair.*) Please step back with me—delicately—to admire. . . .

They step back.

THE MAN and THE WOMAN (*admiring together*): Oh! . . . Oh! . . . Ah! Ah! . . . Oh! Oh! Ah! Ah! . . . Oh! It's simply sublime!

The Arabs who had left the stage re-enter. Very soft music is heard. Perhaps "Tannhäuser" or "La Vie en rose"—one would like to know precisely what. The gilded screen, the dummy, and the characters who were on the second platform remain. Below, in front of the rampart, the Arabs have returned. KADIDJA is present. Enter SIR HAROLD. He leans on the shoulder of his SON, a boy of sixteen or seventeen. He is sad, but resolute. Near KADIDJA is an Arab.

SIR HAROLD: According to a famous and eternal phrase: you're stinking jackals.

KADIDJA *takes* THE ARAB'S *fist and imperiously stuffs it into her mouth.* THE ARAB *withdraws it.*

KADIDJA (*trembling*): Leave your fist in my mug or I'll roar.

THE ARAB *quickly sticks his fist back into her mouth.*

SIR HAROLD (*to his* SON): I've worked all my life to be able to hand this estate down to you, my son. Now all that remains is ashes . . . (*The flags disappear from the top of the screen, so do the characters.*) . . . desolation, silence. The very day she communed with God, your sister died, murdered. But don't be afraid, I won't hurt you. . . . (*He looks about him.*) But . . . I don't see many of your women, or children. . . . Do you fear for them? No? Well then, where are . . . (SIR HAROLD, *who is alone with his* SON, *seems panicky. He continues talking to his* SON; *meanwhile, darkness has set in, or almost.*) My son, when it comes to protecting roses or orange trees, if their roots must be fed with the sweat, saliva, and tears of thousands of men, do not hesitate. A handsome tree is worth more than a fine man, and even a handsome man. Are you armed? (*Sir Harold's* SON *shows the revolver which he has just taken out.*) Good. Yonder will always be France. . . .

KADIDJA (*reappearing, right, and screaming*): . . . and I say that your force is powerless against our hatred . . .

THE ARAB *rushes on-stage and puts his fist back into* KADIDJA's *mouth.*

SIR HAROLD (*to* KADIDJA): What do you mean? It's dark. . . .
THE ARAB: Don't listen to her, she's crazy. . . .
KADIDJA: . . . ashes, desolation, silence, and your little sister . . .

A shot. She falls, supported by THE ARAB. *The shot was fired by Sir Harold's* SON, *who calmly puts his revolver back into his belt. The two men walk off the stage, backwards. Silence.*

THE ARAB (*to the audience*): She's dead.

There is darkness for a few seconds. Then the light returns, but it is very weak. KADIDJA *is alone. She is holding a lighted candle and standing against the screen, right.*

KADIDJA (*in a very severe tone*): I'm dead? So I am. Well, not yet! I haven't finished my job. So, Death, I'll fight it out with you! Saïd, Leila, my loved ones! You, too, in the evening related the day's evil to each other. You realized that in evil lay the only hope. Evil, wonderful evil, you who remain when all goes to pot, miraculous evil, you're going to help us. I beg of you, evil, and I beg you standing upright, impregnate my people. And let them not be idle! (*She calls out in a tone of authority.*) Kaddur! (*After three seconds, an Arab appears. He moves forward from the right wing. He approaches* KADIDJA.) What have you done for evil to prevail?

In the scene that follows, dialogue and gestures will be very rapid, almost as if the characters were rushing each other.

KADDUR (*in a hollow, but proud tone*): Their muzzles are still hot—put your hand on them—look: I picked up two revolvers.
KADIDJA (*curtly*): Set them down there! . . . Their muzzles are smoking . . . the eyelets fierce and grinning. . . .

KADDUR *very quickly draws the revolvers on the screen with a charcoal pencil. Then he goes to the left side of the stage. The drawings should represent the objects monstrously enlarged.*

KADIDJA (*she will speak throughout in the same severe tone*): M'Barek! (*Enter* M'BAREK.) What did *you* do?

M'BAREK: At the stroke of noon, disemboweled three of their cows. And with calf. Here are the horns. (*He draws the horns on the screen and goes to the left side of the stage.*)

KADIDJA: And do everything silently, we're being listened to. Lahussein!

Like the others, LAHUSSEIN *enters from the right. Starting with the following speech, the characters will speak in a violent but muted tone.*

LAHUSSEIN: Under the orange trees, raped one of their girls, I bring you the bloodstain.

He draws the bloodstain, in red, on the screen. The Arabs now enter at a more rapid rate. They wait at the right, eager to appear.)

KADIDJA (*severely*): That's your pleasure and hers. But what about the crime that serves us?

LAHUSSEIN (*loudly*): The one who fucks her after me will never see the eyes with which she looked up at the color of the oranges in the sky.

KADIDJA (*laughing*): Button your fly, boy.

THE WOMAN (*she takes a few steps, outside the set, and leans forward to call, as if she were leaning out of a window*): Monsieur! . . . Monsieur and Madame Bonneuil! . . . Oh, hello! Superb weather, isn't it? Oh! Why, that's wonderful! Oh! Open the window wide. . . . Oh, splendid! (*To her husband*): Georges, come and see Monsieur and Madame Bonneuil's . . . (*Speaking into the wings.*) At what time did you start? You got up at dawn. . . . Very good idea putting some in the hair too. . . .

THE MAN (*leaning forward, like his wife*): The two hanging from the calf, the right calf, what are they? . . . (*A pause.*) Oh, Oh! I didn't know that your family possessed them.

(*A pause.*) We'd love you to. We'll be expecting you.

The husband and wife seem to return to their home. They roll the dummy to the middle of the room.

KADIDJA (*calling out*): Nasser!

NASSER: I yelled "down with the bastards" and my scream fluttered the backdrop stretched across the horizon. And here's my scream!

He draws a screaming mouth, from which a streak emerges, and goes to the left.

KADIDJA: M'Hamed!

M'HAMED: I plucked out the heart. . . .

KADIDJA: Put it down! (M'HAMED *draws the heart and leaves.*) M'Hamed! (*He re-enters.*) That heart looks old.

M'HAMED (*approaching the screen and drawing a few spirals above the heart*): It's still steaming, Kadidja.

KADIDJA: Thank you, my son. (*She calls out.*) Larbi!

LARBI: Opened a paunch to find the guts . . . they're warm. (*He draws the guts, which are also steaming.*)

KADIDJA (*she purses her lips*): Not a nice smell.

LARBI (*annoyed*): Either I leave them here or sew them up again under the skin of the belly.

KADIDJA: Leave them. (*She calls out.*) Mustapha! (*But* LARBI *interrupts her.*)

LARBI (*lyrically*): Blue! . . . pink! . . . green! . . . The blue, the pink, the green—and the crimson—I realized that colors existed when I disemboweled the rural cop. Every color of his guts and shit was warm and entered me through the nose, it warmed my cheeks and the hairy rims of my eyes . . . it . . .

KADIDJA (*peremptorily*): That'll do. . . . Make up a song about it and sing it on the highways. Mustapha!

LARBI *leaves the stage.*

MUSTAPHA (*stepping forward*): Blue eyes of young ladies . . . (*He draws a string of blue eyes.*)

KADIDJA: Ali! (ALI *enters silently and draws a hideous, severed head with a captain's képi. He leaves.*) Kaddur! (KADDUR *enters and draws two hands cut off at the wrist. He leaves.*) Kuider! (*Enter* KUIDER.)

KUIDER: I was afraid. I ran away.

KADIDJA (*forcefully*): Thank you, my son. Draw your jitters! (KUIDER *draws two legs that seem to be running.*) And if any crap ran down your leg, don't forget it. (*She calls out.*) Amer! (*Enter* AMER.)

AMER: Robbed a bank.

KADIDJA: Set down the dough. (AMER *draws a sheaf of banknotes, then stands at the left, with the others.*) Attrache! (*Enter* ATTRACHE.) And you?

ATTRACHE: Dynamited lemon trees.

KADIDJA: Set it down. (ATTRACHE *draws a lemon branch and goes to the left.*) Azuz! (*Enter* AZUZ.) And you?

AZUZ: The sun—the sun or a fireman's helmet that's got to be put out?—the setting sun was too bright, its shadow blinded me, I was sad. . . .

KADIDJA (*smiling*): Go on. But speed up your song and dance. . . .

AZUZ: . . . and I didn't realize the smoke would be so heavy when I struck my safety match. It had rained in the morning, the straw was wet, and it was an almost white smoke that veiled the sun.

KADIDJA (*peremptorily*): Show the embers. Or the ash. Or the flames. Or the smoke. Let it enter me through the nose and fill my windpipe. And let me hear the crackling of the fire. (AZUZ *draws a house in flames, imitates the sound of a crackling fire, then goes to the left.*) Abdesselem! (*Enter* ABDESSELEM.) And you?

ABDESSELEM: Cut off feet!

KADIDJA: Set down the dogs. (ABDESSELEM *draws four feet, very quickly.*) What about the smell? Let's see the smell. . . . (*He draws above them a few spirals of smoke.*) It's strong. (*She calls into the wings.*) You others, come along! Let's go! Come on. Close in. Each must know what the others are doing. And use color! (*The Arabs crowd about and draw on the screen, all at the same time, heads, hands, guns, a few bloodstains. The screen is covered with colored drawings.*)And don't be ashamed, my sons! Merit the world's contempt. Slit throats, my sons. . . .

They continue drawing in silence.

AN ARAB: There's no more room!

KADIDJA (*calling out*): Bring out a new rampart!

From the left wing, rear, emerges a screen similar to the first, crenelated and capped with flags, but the second one is larger and will top the one already on the stage. The Arabs all rush forward (but in very orderly fashion) to cover it with drawings. Meanwhile, up above, the two old people are pinning decorations on the dummies.

THE WOMAN (*appraising*): Not too much light? . . . Draw the curtains a little . . . that's it . . .

THE MAN: They have a very fine one.

THE WOMAN (*sharply*): If it were only up to me, ours would be finer.

THE MAN: Take it easy. My ancestors *also* had something to do with the crop. (*He points to the dummy.*) And if not for me, you'd have only half of it. I brought the family's stuff.

THE WOMAN: You brought half of the family's. Your brother took the other half.

THE MAN: True. But you brought only half of yours. Your sister and brother-in-law have the other.

Enter MONSIEUR *and* MADAME BONNEUIL.

MONSIEUR and MADAME BONNEUIL (*together*): Oh! It's simply admirable! (*They approach and step back, with tiny steps.*) It's simply sublime!

MONSIEUR BONNEUIL (*alone*): You'd have to go a long way to find comparisons! The sea? To open the belly of the oceans, pluck out its fish, its coral? And even then!

MADAME BONNEUIL: Or else rub your eyes till there's sand under your eyelids, and even then!

THE WOMAN: But yours!

MADAME BONNEUIL (*superciliously*): Oh! Ours . . . it's ours!

KADIDJA (*calling out*): Lassen! (*Enter* LASSEN, *right. He is an old man.*) What have *you* done?

LASSEN (*who was the notable clad in silk*): At my age . . . I prayed. . . .

KADIDJA: Thank you, father. Get God in on it. Let him commit his crimes right and left, let him kill, let him pulverize, let him destroy. (*To* LASSEN): Go. Write your prayer on the wall. If you can't find any more crimes, steal crimes from heaven, it's bursting with them! Wangle the murders of the gods, their rapes, their fires, their incest, their lies, their butcheries! Wangle them and bring them! There! (*She points to the wall, which is almost entirely covered with monstrous drawings. Turning to the wings.*) As for the women, let them give birth to monsters!

MADAME BONNEUIL: Have you seen the one of the Trioules?

THE WOMAN: I have it here. I have it in focus. (*She points to the field glass.*)

MONSIEUR BONNEUIL: And what do you make out from here?

THE WOMAN (*installing herself at the field glass, which is fixed on the left wing*): She's pinning . . . pinning . . . pinning . . . the way one peels . . . the way one peels. . . . (*To her husband, without moving her eye from the lens*): Georges, pour Monsieur and Madame Bonneuil some coffee. I've also got the one of the Dumonts in focus. I see some fake ones. And even bow ties. What about you, do you get many?

MADAME BONNEUIL: Many. But we prefer to fix ours in the late afternoon, because of the effects of the sunset.

MONSIEUR BONNEUIL: Bow ties! My poor country! . . .

MADAME BONNEUIL: And we, we leading families, we're lucky to have that. But what of those who have nothing? Everyone has something, true enough, but what of those who have nothing?

THE MAN: It's awful. That's why I invite the most underprivileged to come and contemplate my trophy once a month.

MADAME BONNEUIL: I'd very gladly do the same, if it weren't for the worry of keeping for ourselves the little we have left. And I consider they have enough with the national holiday. Flags in all the windows, even the skylights, and flags of all colors, if you please. I've been told that in the past the national holiday had only three colors, now it has an incalculable number. . . .

THE WOMAN: Like our decorations. Look, they've just pinned on the Grand Merit of Renunciation. . . .

MADAME BONNEUIL: Have they the Valor of the Cross and Saber?

THE WOMAN: They do. And also the medal commemorating the Erection of the Central Bridge. . . .

The ten or twelve Arabs who had entered leave quietly. KADIDJA *watches them go.*

KADIDJA (*to herself*): It's true, there's no room left. . . . (*She yells.*) Hey, kids, snotnoses! (*No sooner is this said than a third screen, larger than the other two, enters alone, left. It is covered with drawings similar to those on the other two.*) All right. Thanks. (*She yells.*) You females! (*A woman enters, right. She is holding a child in her arms.*) Is that you, Srira? Bring in your vermin . . . show him the ramparts . . . let him fill his eyes, his lovely black eyes, with all the beauties of the land! (*Four or five women enter, each carrying a baby, but they remain near the wings. Suddenly everyone is silent. Enter* THE MOTHER. *She smiles. To* THE MOTHER): Well, well, you back? We'd forgotten about you.

THE MOTHER (*shrugging*): And you, you're here! It's written that I'm to spend my nights cheek by jowl with the dead. You too, you haven't been dead long either. Your indignation's still fresh, your blood hasn't stopped flowing.

KADIDJA: What have you been doing?

THE MOTHER: While the men were piling up heads and hearts and severed hands, I kept watch. Leila stole your dresses and coffee grinders, and Saïd helped her.

All the Arabs make a gesture of contempt for her, but KADIDJA *stops them.*

KADIDJA: Continue, and do well what you have to do.

THE MOTHER: I *give* advice, I don't take it. I sow my seed as I like.

KADIDJA: I know you're on intimate terms with what no longer has a name on earth, but you've got to . . .

THE MOTHER (*interrupting her and leaving*): I did that number before my time.

The Arabs angrily drive THE MOTHER *away.*

KADIDJA (*taken aback for a moment, to the Arabs who remain*): And you, is that all you've brought me? Then get the hell out. And don't let her return to the village. Let her ravage! Let her ravage! (*The Arabs leave. A rather long pause.* KADIDJA *is alone. Then, five or six women enter silently.*) Approach! Do you have what's needed?

MADAME BONNEUIL's *voice is heard in the distance.*

MADAME BONNEUIL: What about the Order of the Grand Epileptic, do they have that?

THE WOMAN: They do. And the Sidetrack to God Ribbon? . . .

MADAME BONNEUIL: They do. . . .

HABIBA: I have a sponge and vinegar.

LALLA: Where are you going? Not to die?

KADIDJA: To die. To go to sleep as after a good meal, and belch it all my death. Are you ready?

NEDJMA: I've got the turkish towels. And my gentleness, to close your eyes with.

KADIDJA: It's strength that you'll need in your wrist. Lay me out and wash me well. Without silly chatter. No, don't chase the flies away. I already know them all by name! (*The women begin to bury* KADIDJA.) Don't forget to bind my jaw and stuff cotton in my ears and nostrils and up my ass. I've already been among the dead for three minutes, and I'll see how I can continue to help you . . . because I'm bringing tons of hatred there. . . . Wash my feet well, in particular! . . . it'll be the second time in three years. . . .

SCENE THIRTEEN

The set is as follows: On the stage level, foreground, slightly to the right, is a five-paneled screen representing a field, with a cactus, both painted green. At the foot of the screen, a real milestone, on which nothing can be read. Behind, and high enough so that the character who walks on it is not concealed by the first screen, is a platform on which will enter, when indicated, a second screen. It will remain slightly to the left, upstage. Above this first platform will be a second (there will thus be three levels) onto which a screen will slide, when indicated, from the right.

SAÏD *and* LEILA *enter from behind the screen. They look exhausted. Then, suddenly,* THE GENDARME *appears, right.* THE GENDARME's *uniform is all torn and muddy. His wife, who is in front of him, is pushing a baby carriage loaded with multicolored valises. At the top of the pile is the red cardboard valise* THE MOTHER *was carrying in Scene One.* THE GENDARME *is driving his wife with a cudgel. They very rapidly describe a semicircle, entering at the right and leaving at the left. The woman is wearing dark blue clothes, which are in rags. Her stockings are falling over her heels and we see her pale calves.*

THE GENDARME: Trot! (*He strikes her. She trots.*) My years in the colonial service have taught me to make women trot. I've learned about women from my female disguises and my years in the service! (*He snickers.*)

THE WIFE: You understand things better because you're scared.

THE GENDARME: Being scared also has advantages. And since I'm getting more and more scared, my wits are getting sharper and sharper. (*Roughly.*) Watch out for the cactus! (*He lowers his voice.*) And trot faster and more smoothly. (*Professorially.*) Hearse horses know how to trot. Roll the valises as if you were rolling our dead child.

THE WIFE (*in a gentle tone, and turning around*): Want me to sing them rock-a-bye-baby?

THE GENDARME: When it gets dark. (*He puts out his hand.*) It's already beginning to drizzle. . . . We've got to get away. . . .

The red valise falls and opens. It is empty. THE GENDARME *rushes to pick it up. Then they disappear, left, still trotting.* SAÏD *and* LEILA *emerge from behind the screen.*

SAÏD (*turning around to look at* LEILA): There's not much more you lack: ugly, idiotic, a thief, a beggar, and now a cripple.

LEILA: I can walk straight if I like. (*She walks straight for a few steps.*)

SAÏD (*hastily*): How would I look if all of a sudden you became beautiful, intelligent, honest, dignified, and you walked straight?

They continue walking. After a silence.

LEILA: I'm tired from walking, the sun, the dust. I no longer feel my legs. They've become the road itself. The dust on the road is the sadness of my face that's dropping to my feet. Where are we going, Saïd, where are we going?

SAÏD (*turning around and looking her straight in the eye*): Where am

I going?

LEILA: Where are we going, Saïd?

SAÏD: Where I'm going, me, and me alone, since you're my misfortune and nothing but. Unless when speaking about me and my misfortune I say "we." Well, I'm going, and it must be far away, to the land of the monster. Even if it's where there'll never be sun, since I'm carrying you and dragging you along you're my shadow.

LEILA: You can separate from your shadow.

SAÏD: If you stick to me the way crabs stick to balls, the way roundness sticks to the orange, I've still got to look for the land where the monster lives.

LEILA: Wasn't jail enough for you?

SAÏD: Jail's the beginning. Before long there'll be nothing to sleep on but flint and nothing to eat but thistles. Will you eat that?

LEILA: Thistles?

SAÏD: Flint.

LEILA: There's really nobody. Not a living thing. Nothing. So much so that even the stones are now nothing but stones. And all Europe's no longer anything. Things are shoving off, shoving off, she to the sea, we to the sand.

SAÏD: You've nothing more to be afraid of.

LEILA: I have. (*A pause.*) A piece of mirror. (LEILA, *exhausted, stops. She takes out a comb and is about to comb her hair.*)

SAÏD (*angrily*): Don't touch it. (*He tears the comb from* LEILA'*s hands and breaks it.*)

LEILA: I'll obey you. (*With sudden severity.*) But I want—it's my ugliness, earned hour by hour, that speaks, or what speaks?—I want you to stop looking backward. I want you to lead me without flinching to the land of shadow and of the monster. I want you to plunge into irrevocable grief. I want you—it's my ugliness, earned minute by minute, that speaks—to be without hope. I want you to

choose evil and always evil. I want you to know only hatred
and never love. I want you—it's my ugliness, earned
second by second, that speaks—to refuse the brilliance
of darkness, the softness of flint, and the honey of thistles.
I know where we're going, Saïd, and why we're going
there. It's not just to go somewhere, but so that those
who are sending us there remain tranquil, on a tranquil
shore. We're here, and we're here so that those who are
sending us here realize that they're not here.

A long silence. SAÏD *takes off a shoe and shakes out a stone that has
been bothering him. Then, he puts it on again.*

SAÏD (*gravely*): If I succeed, later on they'll be able to say—
and about anyone, I maintain it without boasting—
"Compared to Saïd, it's a cinch!" I'm telling you, I'm
on my way to becoming someone. Are you coming?

They start walking again. Then LEILA *stops.*

LEILA: I have to go, Saïd.
SAÏD (*coldly*): Go do it in the nettles.
LEILA: I came to an understanding with them long ago.
We're of the same breed. I place my ass quietly in
their bouquet, they don't give me a rash. (*Sadly.*) There
are nettles, and nothing else. (*She has gone behind the
screen. We hear her say.*) A used match is pretty. It's only
then, when it's white and black and a little twisted by
the flame, that it looks gentle and kind.
SAÏD (*who has just picked up two stones and now suddenly strikes
them together*): Watch out! Someone's coming. Don't say
anything, not even hello.

Enter Sir Harold's SON *and* THE VAMP, *left. She is dressed in black, like a Venetian woman, with a triangular hat and a veil that is draped across her face like a scarf. Long dress. She is holding above her head a small, black lace parasol. But her whole outfit is in tatters.* THE VAMP *and* THE SON *seem ready to drop with fatigue.* LEILA *comes out from behind the screen, arranging her skirt.*

THE VAMP: As if I were utterly worthless . . . you talk to me as if I were a streetwalker. . . . You used to . . .

THE SON: *I* need something tangible. My mind won't be at rest till our peace and order are restored in this land, but for the time being we've got ot keep our eyes peeled. (*Suddenly.*) Watch out, Madame, there's a bush moving. . . .

THE VAMP: With you I fear nothing.

THE SON (*Looking at* SAÏD *and* LEILA): They look even seedier than we. . . . Maybe we can bulldoze them. . . .

THE VAMP: It's awfully hot.

THE SON (*to* SAÏD): Did you hear? Make some shade for Madame, and be quick about it. . . .

SAÏD *kicks* LEILA, *who approaches the screen and, very slowly and carefully, draws with green chalk a magnificent palm tree.*

THE VAMP: (*admiringly*): Oh! Palms!

THE SON (*to* LEILA): Make a little breeze for Madame. . . .

With her mouth, LEILA *simulates the sound of wind in the branches, and with her skirt, the rush of air.*

THE VAMP (*blandly*): Thank you. I told you so: there are some lovely ones among the lot. Not everything's rotten. Those, for example (*Pointing to* SAÏD *and* LEILA.), they're no doubt supporters of ours.

THE SON: Got to wipe out the lot of them. Supporters, yes,

so they seem, if all one looks at is their rags, but underneath? . . . What's underneath? Even *I* don't dare go
and look. . . . A bunch of grenades. . . . A nest of machine
guns . . . A center of infection. . . .

THE VAMP: With a little kindness . . . no, no, believe me, it
wouldn't take much. . . .

THE SON: They don't give a damn about kindness. They still
make shade, true enough, when you force them, but
it's not the shade it used to be.

THE VAMP (*straightening up*): It's true that this one is disturbing.

THE SON: Have you rested a little? . . . You know I love you
and that you're everything to me. . . .

THE VAMP (*interrupting him with a gentle smile*): That's how a
young man in our sphere ought to talk when he's hot
in the pants for me. But if we continue on our way,
on the rocky road, beneath the sun, in our tatters, and
beneath the astonished gaze of *that* (*Pointing to* SAÏD *and*
LEILA.), we'll also have to continue with that awful
language.

THE SON: You're right, it gives *me* a pain in the ass too, but
if we want to clear out fast, words have to get jittery,
just like us. Let's get going.

THE VAMP (*moving to the right*): To think that even the softest
carriage seats used to be too hard for my ass. . . .

THE SON: Before setting eyes on the sky-blue sea, you'll have
to get used to lots of hardships.

They leave, right. LEILA, *who had remained motionless in the sun,
tries to stand up.*

SAÏD: Here comes night.

LEILA: Already?

SAÏD: Look. It sure is sure of itself!

He points to the second screen, all black, which glides softly along the platform, behind the first screen. The darkness comes on gently, downstage. A lot of barking is heard, off-stage: it is an imitation by THE MOTHER.

SAÏD (*to* LEILA): Rest your head against the milestone and try to sleep.

LEILA: (*stretching out at the foot of the milestone*): Sleep? If I scratch the soles of my feet on the flint, if I eat thistles, if I let myself be beaten by the sun, it's in order to murder the dragon of my sleep.

SAÏD: Since you know it won't croak till the second of your death, let me snooze. Up there, let God do his job. . . .

Crouching at the foot of the screen, he falls asleep. The barking is heard again. Then, THE MOTHER *enters, left, on the platform.*)

THE MOTHER (*she seems to be calling something invisible. Then, she runs after it*): So I'm Laughter planted on two big feet in the dead of night deep in the countryside. I want to be seen more clearly! (*With yellow chalk, she draws a crescent moon on the black screen. Then, she moves a step or two nearer the audience. To the moon*): Hello! I'm Laughter —not just any laughter, but the kind that appears when all goes wrong. (*She looks at the audience.*) It's the night full of nettles. (*A pause.*) Nettles! (*Suddenly lyrical.*) Through the lords of old, go back to the Fairy, back to the Virgin, I, I've known since childhood that I belong—perhaps through the females, and Saïd through me—to the nettle family. Near ruins, tangled with shards, their bushes were my cruelty, my hypocritical meanness that I kept, with one hand behind my back, in order to hurt the world! I tamed them and they held in their venom, drew in their needles. In their leaves I steeped my delicate

hands: hemlock would not have frozen my veins. Everything wicked in the vegetable kingdom was won over to
me. When the wind blew over and through the nettles,
it scraped its skin, but not I. But what of the white nettle?
Ah! Not only was it harmless, but its white flowers were
good and I made soup with them. (*She walks silently for
a moment, then disappears. The moon also disappears. Several
barks are heard. Then* THE MOTHER *reappears, and with her
the crescent moon, but turned in the other direction. With sudden
sternness.*) So, my fair Kadidja, you're dead! Kicked the
bucket! Kicked it heroically. And if I wanted to talk
to you, would I have to use the old Mouth of the dead
again? But . . . you died doing what? Rousing the men
and women to go the limit? They'll all go to the limit
of what they're doing, and what they're becoming!
(*She laughs.*) One sees the path! You think you've got
me because you set fire to my shanty, my garbage can.
I'm stronger than you think. I'd have the strength,
me with my wrestler's forearms, to cleave the Red Sea
and make a path for the Pharaoh! (*A pause.*) Saïd?
Leila? Have they fallen asleep on the road? (*A pause.*)
Saïd's father could have been a barber. . . . So handsome
he was almost blond. (*A pause.*) Beauty! Too beautiful
to be true. If for twenty years you remained on earth,
O Beauty, it's because my man so wished. (*A very long
silence, during which she scratches her thighs. Suddenly a burst
of machine-gun fire.*) It took three tries to produce Saïd.
Botched, all three of them. Died. Died at the age of six
months, a year, and three months. (*Suddenly she seems
uneasy.*) What? What is it? A sprint setting in the shape
of a rabbit, a flight in the shape of a bat . . . (*Panicky.*)
Saïd! Saïd! Where are you? What are you doing?
What are you saying? . . . You're out of breath. . . . Come
back. . . . (*A pause.*) No, go further, Saïd. Demolish

yourself and demolish your wife, but carry on. . . . (*She seems to grow calmer; she is breathing slowly.*) At night, the trees breathe, the flowers are lovelier, the colors warmer, and the village sleeps. (*She laughs.*) What does it do? It merges in its brotherhood. (*She laughs.*) While snoring away, everyone prepares the nightmare into which he'll plunge on awakening. (*A pause.*) Ah! If only the she-dog that lives in my belly could have gone prowling at night, in the farmyards and along the roads!

THE MOTHER *resumes her way, slowly, and disappears behind the black screen. Another burst of machine-gun fire. A ray of light settles on* LEILA's *face.* SAÏD *is examining her with a pocket flashlight.*

SAÏD: Has he come?

LEILA: He's drawing near.

SAÏD: Already! (*A pause.*) Ask him . . . (*He hesitates.*) . . . ask him what I can say, what I can sell out on, so as to be a complete louse.

LEILA (*in a choked tone*): Ask my dragon?

SAÏD (*humbly*): Yes.

LEILA (*after a hesitation*): Then let me go back to sleep. And you'll know tomorrow what he told me.

SAÏD *puts out his flashlight and goes back to sleep.* THE BANKER *and* SIR HAROLD, *both in rags, enter very cautiously from behind the lower screen. They are visibly drunk. In order to pass the sleeping* LEILA *and* SAÏD, *they take off their shoes, then disappear, left. Then, up above, on the third platform, coming from the left, appears the third screen. It will represent a mountainous region. Four Legionnaires have just entered. One of them,* HELMUT, *is cleaning his rifle.* PIERRE *is polishing a shoe.* FELTON *is drinking from a small bottle. All this taken place noiselessly. The gestures imply that it is nighttime. The men speak in a muffled tone.*

PIERRE (*spitting on his shoe and rubbing*): All right, we get it: on the Q.T., pianissimo, in short, dirty tactics, that's how they act. They come up behind us, veiled. When the job's done, they're metamorphosed on the spot. The guy becomes a tree, an eggplant, who knows! What do you do? Pick it up and crush it? You're just picking and crushing an eggplant. The rebel's got away.

MORALES (*standing up*): To say nothing of the fact that their women . . .

PIERRE: All right, we get it: deriving from the reptile, the feline, and thin air. Slippery, light, lithesome. Result: poisonous bites, doses of clap.

FELTON (*laughing*): And how they smell!

PIERRE: Rotten inside, dry outside. In their bellies, swamps. From their mouths, malaria. And seasickness. And they scratch themselves. So why be shy? Wipe 'em out, all of 'em, to the last man. Helmut's right. (*He opens his collar.*) And to begin with, rage wears me out.

MORALES: What time is it?

HELMUT (*looking at his wristwatch*): 11:08.

MORALES *draws, on the screen, a moon at the horizon, then sits down to lace his shoes.*

MORALES: My dogs are barking.

HELMUT: Trash, they're trash, attention!

The four of them spring to attention. Enter THE LIEUTENANT, *right. He looks at the soldiers one after the other, at some length. He touches* PIERRE's *open collar with his switch.*

THE LIEUTENANT: Close it! . . . Good . . . no, close it better . . . the tie . . . tie the knot correctly. Or before you know it you'll have the pale belly of an alligator. No, I wasn't

listening, but a leader knows—one worthy of the name
—the inner thoughts of his . . . no mirrors? Should always
have one; either the eyes of your comrades or . . . look
at yourself in there. (*Pointing to his own tie, he plants himself
in front of* PIERRE, *who knots his tie while pretending to look
at himself in a mirror.*) Fine. Too bad I have to reprimand
you. I quite realize it's not easy in the darkness, but even
in the darkness you've got to shine. To gleam. (*He looks
about him.*) No sergeant?

PIERRE: He's sleeping, Sir.

THE LIEUTENANT (*curtly*): Three. For having informed against
one of your leaders. There remains in the army a tradition
of chivalry, and it's for you to perpetuate it. And let
it glow, Goddamn it! Three. And I don't mean three
of hearts. If no one had answered, each of you would
have got three days in prison for refusal to obey. A charge
less vile than informing. (*To the others*): His ignominy
saves you and besmirches you. French?

PIERRE: Sir?

THE LIEUTENANT: I'm asking whether you're an Arab?

PIERRE: Me? From Boulogne, Sir.

THE LIEUTENANT: The half-tints of the Orient rub off on you,
don't they, its pastel tones cake on you. We represent
a France clear and sharp. (*A pause.*) And clean. Clean,
I say. (*Pointing to* MORALES.) . . . your beard?

MORALES: No water left, Sir.

THE LIEUTENANT: Perhaps not for rinsing your mouth or
sprinkling the geraniums. For shaving, there'll always
be some. Spit on the brush, but I want you smooth-shaven.
Pumiced. (*To* MORALES): Arab?

MORRALES: Me?

THE LIEUTENANT: Shave. (*The soldier takes a shaving brush and
piece of soap from his knapsack. He drains off a little wine
that remains in his canteen, and, standing in front of a rock*

that he has drawn on the screen, shaves himself. THE LIEUTENANT
turns to PIERRE.) I'm canceling your three days in prison.
Since the attack's scheduled for tonight. . . . (*Enter* THE
SERGEANT. *He yawns, then tidies his hair with his hand and
buckles his belt.*) . . . I was saying . . . is scheduled for
tonight. Since, very probably, we won't live to tell the
tale and since an officer can't die on the field of honor
with a jailbird. . . . (*To* PIERRE): Besides, I recognize
you, always lagging behind (*He seems to grow less sure
of himself as he goes on. He steals a glance at* THE SERGEANT,
who still has a merry look in his eye.), you'll be either the last
survivor who casually turns up and collects the glory, or the
first man picked off by a little girl, and in two hours,
no later, lying in the dust, you'll display your ultimate
mutilation to heaven. I'm thirsty. Let me have a drink.
(PIERRE *goes behind the screen.* THE LIEUTENANT *continues,
addressing the others.*) It won't be long now. (*He draws a
mountainous landscape on the screen and comments.*) We're
here . . . beyond the big cedar . . .(*He draws it.*) . . . at
the right, part of the column will march on the village
(*He draws it.*), will by-pass it and then fan out, in
order to get to the top of the hill . . . (*He draws it.*) where
it's to arrive the very minute of dawn. France is watching
us. She's sending us out to die. (*To* FELTON): Comb your
hair. (FELTON *takes a comb from his revolver pocket and combs
his hair.*) It's not a matter of returning victoriously.
What would be the point? (*While he talks, everyone busies
himself, so that* THE LIEUTENANT *seems to be speaking in a void,
with fixed gaze.* MORALES *shaves,* FELTON *combs his hair,*
HELMUT *cleans his bayonet,* THE SERGEANT *files his nails.*)
. . . France has already conquered, that is, she has offered
an indelible image. Therefore, not conquer, but die.
Or half-die, that is, return crippled, armless, legless,
broken and bent, balls torn off, noses eaten away, faces

blasted. . . . That's very fine too. Painful, but very fine. Thus, in the image of its rotting warriors France will be able to watch itself rot. . . . But conquer? . . . And conquer what? Or whom? You've seen them dragging in the mud, living on peelings . . . conquer that! (*Shrugging his shoulders and making, with open palms, the gesture of a Levantine merchant.*) Conquer, that's all right for them. (*In the direction of* THE SERGEANT.) Isn't that so? (THE SERGEANT *yawns and shrugs.*)

A long baying is heard. THE MOTHER *reappears, left, on the level below.*

THE MOTHER (*furiously. The invisible tree to which she is speaking must be made "visible" by her gestures*): Step aside so I can pass, damn it, or I'll tear off your skin, you leafy tree, I'll tear off the skin of your belly strip by strip. (*She makes the gesture of pushing aside the invisible tree.*) Don't you see my skirts, and that they're wide? Didn't skimp on material: four yards of blue cotton. Step aside! So I can pass. There's shade in my skirts just as in yours, and nobility and even an old nest. (*She walks by, with great dignity. Then she turns around and bows.*) Thank you. . . . Hilly country. (*She turns around again and bows.*) Thank you. Your breath'll clear my windpipe, eucalyptus, will swell my lungs, my breath and my phrases and perhaps the she-dog that I am only to myself will become a bitch to you! . . . (*She goes to the right and squats, munching an imaginary leaf which she has just torn off* [*when turning around*]. *Then, she seems to doze. While she was speaking, the four soldiers went off, left.*)

THE LIEUTENANT (*still at attention; to* THE SERGEANT): Has the patrol returned? At what time and in what state?

THE SERGEANT (*coming to attention, then relaxing*): Excuse me, Sir, but when I stand at attention I feel like a dope and what I . . .

THE LIEUTENANT (*anxiously, and at attention*): Do you stretch in order to be more intelligent?

THE SERGEANT: Yes.

THE LIEUTENANT: So that if I put my hands in my pockets in the presence of the Captain I'll become as intelligent as you when you yawn?

THE SERGEANT (*smiling, and bending down to lace a shoe*): Why not?

THE LIEUTENANT (*taken aback for a moment*): It's not a matter of intelligence, but of perpetuating an image that's more than ten centuries old, that grows stronger and stronger as that which it represents crumbles, that leads us all, as you know, to death. (*Crying out.*) Attention! THE SERGEANT *continues lacing his shoe.*) Has the patrol returned?

THE SERGEANT: Except for one man. Strangled.

THE LIEUTENANT: Which one?

THE SERGEANT (*still bent over*): Duval, a waiter, waiter in ·a restau . . . (*His position is uncomfortable.*)

THE LIEUTENANT: . . . rant! There are no waiters in the army. (*He turns toward the wing.*) Let every man be a mirror to every other man. A pair of legs must look at themselves and see themselves in the pair of legs opposite, a torso in the torso opposite, the mouth in another mouth, the eyes in the eyes, the nose in the nose, the teeth in the teeth, the knees in the knees, a curl in . . . another curl, or, if the hair opposite is stiff, in a spit-curl. . . . (*Very lyrically.*) Must look at oneself there and see oneself there supremely handsome . . . (*He about-faces in military fashion and speaks, facing the audience.*) . . . utterly seductive. And let the three-faced mirrors keep multiplying, the

ten-faced, the thirteen, the hundred-thirteen, the thousand,
the hundred-thousand! Let the profiles reflect profiles
back and forth and let the image you offer the rebels
be of such beauty that the image they have of themselves
cannot resist. Conquered, it'll fall to pieces. Broken . . .
or like ice, melted. Victory over the enemy, a moral one.
(THE SERGEANT *strides about very nonchalantly. Standing alone,*
THE LIEUTENANT *continues his monologue in a raging tone.*)
A curl in the curl opposite; the heart in the heart opposite;
the foot in the foot; the nose in the nose; the foot in the
nose; the eye in the teeth . . . (*He seems to be in an actual
state of trance.*) . . . the liver in the liver; the blood in the
blood; the nose bloody, the soup with milk, the soup with
blood . . . Sergeant, Sergeant, perhaps you don't need
all these artifices, Sergeant, you're aware of the power
over yourself of your physique and of the coldness of
your eyes; you're radiant and the devasting taste of
intelligence makes you stick your hands deep down in
your pockets and I who wanted to learn to play the
violin! (*He suddenly springs to attention.*) Reporting for
duty, General! (*A pause.*) Reporting for duty! (*He leaves
right.* THE SERGEANT *remains standing, motionless.*)
THE MOTHER (*loudly, as if she were yelling*): . . . Or the sea! . . .
The trees know a thing or two about it, the hussies! . . .
(*She mutters.*) that carriages drive cartloads of corpses
over the beaches, patience! . . . to go through the woods,
the forests, the darkness, I . . . the . . . Most High Mother
and not yet on the retired list . . . I . . . (*She cries out.*)
foresaw it all! . . . All! (*She keeps walking.*) That's how
it is . . . (*She cocks her ear.*) . . . a machine gun? (*She laughs
and imitates a burst of machine-gun fire.*) There. (*Sternly.*)
There's a horizontal sound. (*She sits on her haunches and
mops her face with a handkerchief, then continues.*) Lunatics
are allowed only words. (*She spits.*) Their nails are cut

off: they scratch. Their hair's cut off: they make ropes
with it. Their nuts are cut off: they stick 'em up their
ass. I trotted in the grass sniffing the traces of a hare. . . .
In winter, I lapped up the water of rain puddles, in
summer my mouth was so dry I couldn't bark.

A VOICE (*rather gently*): Who is it that's speaking?

THE MOTHER: A thorn dragging about.

A VOICE: Thorn or barbed wire?

THE MOTHER: Barbed wire.

THE MOTHER *goes behind the screen. The stage remains empty for a
moment. Then, enter* PIERRE, *left. He lumbers in, as if fatigued.
He is carrying a very heavy bag and his machine gun. He is holding
his shoes by the laces and carrying a glass of water. He sits down
on the stone, while the constellation of the Big Dipper appears on the
screen in the place of the moon.*

PIERRE: Christ! Even the stone is tired. . . . (*He puts down the
glass of water. A pause.*) Damn it to hell, I wonder what
asses, what Goddamned asses could have been sitting
on it? Whereas in Boulogne . . . (*Very proudly.*) to think
that I'm from Boulogne, where the kings met on the
Field of the Cloth of Gold! Every word is written in
capitals. And that means the cloth wasn't of silver, but
of gold. Like my back tooth. And here am I sitting in
the Moslem darkness with the Lieutenant's glass of
water! (*He stands up with difficulty and continues walking
toward the left. He is about to leave the stage and go behind
the screen when the voice of* THE MOTHER—*very loud—is
heard off-stage.*)

THE MOTHER: There's no more moon! . . . Funny place! . . .
Really, no more moon. The moon has betrayed its
mission! . . . Betrayed? But who betrays? (*She enters*

from the right wing.) Nowadays, no one. Betrayal . . . Betrayal . . . the poor little word, poor little word lying there all alone, lost, without anyone to pick it up, to warm it? . . . Hello, who's there? . . . What is it, who is it? . . . a man? Is it a man? . . . Who's there? Approach. Even at my age I can still recognize a man's fly. Let's see you. (PIERRE *heaves, as if he were about to vomit.*) Are you puking?

PIERRE (*in a hollow voice*): I couldn't hold it in any more. I had to relieve myself.

THE MOTHER (*going up to him and supporting his head*): There's all kinds of stuff in it: old omelette and red wine. . . .

PIERRE: That's right.

THE MOTHER: Let yourself go. . . . Keep on, if you want to. . . . Maybe it's the dizzying beauty of the panorama that turned your stomach. That's been known to happen.

PIERRE (*wiping his mouth with his sleeve*): But you, what are you doing here at this hour?

THE MOTHER: I came to relieve myself in the dirt. Where are you from?

PIERRE: Boulogne . . . (*A pause.*) You're not spying on us, are you?

THE MOTHER (*still supporting him*): I'm singing and laughing at the thought that it's you who'll be the death of us all. If you manage to turn the village into a little red blood-stain on the map . . .

PIERRE: We'll do what we can. Help me on with my pack.

Still supporting him, THE MOTHER *puts the knapsack around his neck, but she notices that she has wound the strap around twice. She tries to free him. This goes on for some time. A shot and a dull thud are heard.*

PIERRE: See that?

THE MOTHER (*continuing her work*): Heard it.

PIERRE (*sure of himself*): That's the General rolling down the depths of time.

THE MOTHER: He or someone else and there or elsewhere . . . Sorry . . . I was never good at harnessing soldiers . . . I no longer know right from left.

PIERRE *also starts twisting and gets tangled in the straps.*

PIERRE: The Lieutenant's waiting for his drink of water. Make it snappy. Pull back the knapsack from the front. . . .

THE MOTHER (*still busily arranging the straps*): But which is the front, the back, the belly, the ass, the bottom, the top? Here or there? . . . Everywhere else? (*As she speaks, she rolls straps, which keep getting longer, more numerous and tighter.*) The right side, the wrong side? . . . the hot and the cold? . . . Where is true North, false South? . . .

PIERRE (*slightly anxious*): Say, granny . . . you playing a game or something? You're too old for that. . . . What're you doing?

THE MOTHER (*panting*): Knots . . . bags . . . bags of knots . . . buckles and cross-belts . . . knitted caps. . . .

PIERRE (*in a weak tone and struggling*): Granny? What are you. . . .

THE MOTHER (*suddenly losing patience, she vigorously pulls the strap, pressing her knee against the soldier's back*): I'm pulling. (*She imitates the sound of a machine gun, then spits in her hands and pulls harder.*)

PIERRE: You're kidding around, granny . . . .

THE MOTHER: I sometimes do. . . . (*She pulls again.*) . . . I just did . . . (THE SOLDIER *falls, with his tongue hanging out.* THE MOTHER *straightens up and stands for a moment, catching her breath.*) I just did. (*With sudden panic.*) It's not possible? You haven't done that, have you, old girl? . . . spoiled an entire life? (*She gives the corpse a kick.*) It's not true, you're not dead? Stand up. On your feet! You're not dead. I didn't kill you, did I? (*She kneels beside the corpse.*) Answer me, I beg you, answer, little soldier of France, love, my love, my pussycat, my little mousie, stand up . . . come on, up, you trash! (*She straightens up and picks up the belt.*) He's dead all right, the swine! And what does one do with these things? (*She starts dragging the corpse as one drags a piece of dead game.*) What is it I'm dragging? Why those belts around its silky neck? (*She stops to catch her breath.*) The blood didn't spurt to the sky like a geyser, yet from one edge of the world to the other how red the night is!

She turns around and, imitating the sound of a machine gun, aims at the corpse with her hand. She disappears behind the black screen, dragging the body. This level remains empty for a moment. Then, groping in the darkness, appear THE LIEUTENANT *and* THE GENERAL. *They seem not to notice* THE SERGEANT, *who is standing motionless.*

THE GENERAL (*replying to something* THE LIEUTENANT *must have asked off-stage*): . . . Eleven. July 20th. He'll be eleven years old. (*A pause.*) Whether I'll ever see him again . . . whether he'll ever see me again? . . . As a ward of the army, he'll enter the Military Academy. But he won't have a career in the Colonial Troops. . . . (*Sadly.*) There won't be any Colonial Troops since there won't be any colonies, won't be any Foreign Legion since there won't be any foreigners. Everything'll be flat. Are you limping? (*They will advance very slowly, bent forward, one behind the other, groping. All their gestures must make us feel the darkness.*)

THE LIEUTENANT: My foot's still sprained.

THE GENERAL: Going down the steps of the mess hall? I'd suggested putting up a banister. A rope, a simple rope.

Oh well . . . it's not humiliating for an officer to limp. Less than if he coughed. (*A pause.*) No, won't be any colonies. My son may reach manhood without knowing what a native is. Or else, he has no time to lose. Our opponents are fighting too. And the fight improves their looks . . . have you noticed?

THE LIEUTENANT: You too? Bend forward. Your back's above the ridge.

THE GENERAL (*in the tone of a shopkeeper who sees his customers dwindling*): Fewer and fewer sneaky looks . . . fewer and fewer shifty faces . . . (*Gravely.*) Lieutenant, beware of that waxing beauty. (*Lyrically.*) Beauty, beauty, brick-and-mortar of armies, as you say, brick-and-mortar for us but for them too. (*A pause.*) I'm wondering, after twenty-eight years in the service, if I hadn't admired my martial bearing in a mirror would I have been brave enough to defend it? . . . If ever *they* get their hands on a mirror. . . .

THE LIEUTENANT: I've given orders to fire first on the mirrors. Besides, nothing's left of the village. Our friends have been killed or have fled. The others . . .

THE GENERAL: They've taken so much shit they can't hold it in any more. We'll be walking in it, and if we don't have new techniques . . . (*A sigh.*) Beauty, brick-and-mortar of armies . . . That's one of your phrases, isn't it? What about Sergeant what's-his-name?

THE LIEUTENANT (*as if seeing the light*): I realize why they no longer steal the sneakers of our dead.

THE GENERAL: What about the Sergeant? You don't say a word about him.

THE LIEUTENANT: To say nothing of the fact that that maddening Saïd, who still can't be found, keeps getting worse and worse. A traitor . . .

THE GENERAL: It's thanks to his treason that our men—I'm

talking like a broad!—managed to capture the rock where we are.

THE LIEUTENANT: And the more disgusting and repulsive he is . . .

THE GENERAL (*with sudden anger*): What about the Sergeant? You're afraid to talk about him. He's getting more and more handsome, I hope?

THE LIEUTENANT: Loaned to the special section. (*A pause.*) I'll have it massaged . . .

THE GENERAL (*severely*): Got the shakes? (*He sings softly.*) Beauty, brick-and-mortar . . . The Sergeant knows how to bring that splendor to a head! Admit he's got you scared.

THE LIEUTENANT (*in a humble tone*): I didn't think one could go that far. . . . I hadn't had occasion to see so handsome a monster at close range. I admit I drew back, but I'm going to buck up. . . .

THE GENERAL: Drew back? . . . Buck up? . . . Drew back where, buck up what? Yet it's he who's become our model, whether we like it or not. When a challenge is accepted, you've got to go through with it, unto damnation. And when it's against the Infidel, we've got to rouse within us the chaste cruelty of the Saracen Chronicles. . . . The Sergeant . . .

THE LIEUTENANT (*in a hollow tone*): He even kills children . . . little girls . . .

THE GENERAL (*admiringly*): Little Saracen girls! Too late to draw back. That sergeant's an Excalibur and he thrusts to the hilt!

THE LIEUTENANT: His neck . . . his teeth . . . his smile . . . and especially his gaze . . . He kills so well, so coldly, because he's in power. His beauty protects him. . . .

THE GENERAL: And protects us . . .

THE LIEUTENANT: . . . about us.

THE GENERAL (*crossly*): What's that you say?

THE LIEUTENANT: His Beauty doesn't give a damn about us. There's also the fact that he knows he's loved, he feels he's loved by us, and already pardoned. And we, we have no one. . . .

THE GENERAL (*in a severe tone*): Our leaders have always encouraged us to regard ourselves as perfect objects, ever more perfect, hence more insensitive, wonderful death-dealing machines. Awareness of our solitude gave us this power and the power added to our solitude . . . The Sergeant . . .

THE LIEUTENANT: I didn't think one could go . . .

THE GENERAL (*relentlessly*): Stop the bullshit. One *has* to go. Armed, in boots and helmets, right, but also powdered, cosmeticked, made up, the thing that kills is grease paint on a skeleton of precise gestures, and when death has killed us. . . .

A burst of machine-gun fire. THE GENERAL *falls just as he is about to go behind the screen.* THE LIEUTENANT *crouches. It is in this position that he leaves, dragging the corpse of* THE GENERAL *by the feet, but first he says a few words.*

THE LIEUTENANT (*to the corpse*): No sooner said than done. (*A pause.*) Sir, with all due respect . . . (*He is almost murmuring.*) I'm obliged to tell you that even to knock off an Infidel one has to engage in such theatrical labor that one cannot be both actor and director. . . . (*Another burst of machine-gun fire.*) . . . Damn it, it's raining. (*He draws the corpse by the feet.*) I'm going to have to take your revolver and toss you over . . . and may the General roll down the depths of time.

SCENE FOURTEEN

Two screens. First screen: directly on the floor of the stage, left. It represents the brothel. Second screen: on a platform which can be reached from the floor by a visible staircase, right. It represents the village watering trough. There is no one on this platform when the scene begins in front of the first screen. A bicycle is resting against the second screen, the upper one. And behind this screen project the screens that were covered with drawings in Scene Twelve.

The characters: The soldiers who enter the brothel are Arab fighters. The men who will appear in front of the second screen, that is, the watering trough, are all crippled or disfigured. SRIR *is wearing a mask which makes him look disfigured;* SALEM *is missing an arm (a woman is rolling a cigarette for him);* HAMED *is leaning on a crutch; he is missing a leg;* BACHIR *wears a big bandage on his left arm.*

Costumes: Multicolored, in keeping with the style already indicated. DJEMILA *will wear a mauve dress, white stockings and shoes, a yellow hat. The Arab soldiers: lean, tanned faces, American uniforms, wide-brimmed felt hats, the kind worn, I think, in Texas.*

WARDA (*she stands in front of the mirror; to herself*): I've got a
   bellyache to the very bowels of the earth. The last to

arrive—if he arrives— is going to topple at the edge of a lake. Poor golden petticoats! I'd always hoped that one day, instead of being an adornment, you'd be, by yourselves, the whore in all her glory. A pipe dream. And picking my teeth with hatpins, my style! When I'm tumbled on the bed, it's you, my skirts, that are crushed and creased. Those gentlemen no longer have the strength to lift your leaded hem, and in order for them not to waste time I've had to cut a slit for them in front. (*She lights a cigarette.*) In the brocade a shutter that opens on the bowels of the earth! (*She takes a puff.*) And I had to learn to smoke at the age of forty-two!

The Arab soldier, who is buttoning his shirt collar, leaves the stage, left. Before disappearing, he loads his machine gun. Enter MALIKA, *knotting her belt and tidying her hair.*

MALIKA: We've lost our zest, I for my work and they for pleasure. They go upstairs with their teeth clenched. (*She squats and takes her work basket. She sews.*)
WARDA (*bitterly*): Whereas the women smile at us. (*She smokes.*) I labored within my darkness, to be only a kind of gilded dummy that scrapes its gums with plated pins and now the women invite us with smiling mouths. (*A pause.*) They still haven't the nerve to call me by my name, as their brothers and cousins do. . . . (*She spits out the butt, resentfully.*)

Enter an Arab soldier; WARDA *and he go behind the screen.*

MALIKA: Your turn. Better to drift with the tide. . . . (*She sews.*) If only the sun doesn't dry up the village water supply, if it does what'll we wash with? (*A pause.*) The platoon'll be down again around eight o'clock . . . those who are alive to tell the tale. It'll be rush hour. We'll be mobbed. (*She chuckles.*) I admit they know how to work up there, in the hills! . . . Even in the Bible there've never been such smart killers . . . such valiant killers. . . . (*She chuckles again.*) I wouldn't want to be the daughter, or mother, or wife, or grandmother, or granddaughter of a Frenchman who falls into the hands of our warriors! (*She chuckles.*) I wouldn't dare go and lay celluloid flowers on his grave. (*Re-enter the Arab soldier with his gun.*) You going back up there?

THE SOLDIER: If I came to relieve myself, it wasn't in order to retire on a pension.

MALIKA: Isn't the war enough for you?

THE SOLDIER: *You've* got nothing to complain about.

MALIKA: I'm asking a question. . . .

THE SOLDIER (*after hesitating*): I'm fighting the war to win it. (*A slight pause.*) The fun mustn't be *in* the war, but *beside* it.

He finishes buttoning himself and leaves. MALIKA *shrugs.* WARDA *appears.*

MALIKA: One can hear the water flowing when you wash yourself. You make a splash. . . .

WARDA (*curtly. She goes to the mirror*): I do the job fast. It's a regular factory. They're killing us, at least let's take advantage. Got to rake it in. Bye-bye to my hatpins for picking my teeth. My style! Bye-bye, my style! Men used to come from far away to see me, *me, Warda*, pick my teeth with my big hatpins. Now they come to fuck me.

MALIKA: Fortunately they're willing to pay.

WARDA (*turning around, furiously*): You think they'd have the nerve? . . . They're murdering us! It's like working in a steam bath! . . . They come pouring in under my golden skirts, they rummage in my twists and turns, and even fall asleep there—the number of them who fall asleep there, overcome with drowsiness or fear!—with no respect for my riches or for what I've become in twenty-four years—and then not cough up!

MALIKA: When they come to the surface again, it's in order to go to death. They could . . .

WARDA (*with rising fury*): But we could shut up shop, become nurses. . . . (*A pause.*) You feel it too—that the air and the space and the time now circulating about us are like any other. The brothel's no longer the brothel and, so to speak, we're fucking in the open.

Enter an Arab soldier loaded with machine guns. He goes behind the screen, where MALIKA *follows him. At the second screen, which represents the watering trough, appears* OMMU. *She is holding a kind of empty sachet in her hand. She looks at* HAMED *insolently. Then,* NEDJMA *enters.*

WARDA (*to herself*): A whore! I, Warda, who was to fade away and leave in my place only a perfect whore, a simple skeleton draped in gilded gowns, here am I becoming Warda again at top speed. (*Uttering a long wail, she starts tearing her dress. By the time* MALIKA *arrives, she will be in rags.*)

Above, OMMU, HAMED *and* SRIR *have just entered from behind the screen.*

OMNU (*an Arab woman of about sixty*): Green, pale green, a kind of green glass powder, a green bottle broken and ground; that was it. A packet of it in each well. . . .

HAMED: What about the donkeys? . . . And the sheep?

OMMU: If they don't like arsenic, they can croak. But they won't be the only ones. The handsome blond soldiers will croak with them.

HAMED: There're three disemboweled goats in the Kaddur orange grove, been lying there since yesterday. They're black with fleas. With fleas, with flies. Their bellies burst open in the sun. The worms are gnawing their guts. Your arsenic's no good against fleas and flies. To say nothing of the fact that we may have been betrayed, and in all probability by Saïd. . . .

SRIR: We're heading for catastrophe. If those gentlemen don't find water, they still have water trucks, but what about us?

OMMU (*contemptuously*): All right, go on! Join the Foreign Legion. You'll have not only water but lemonade, and I who haven't even enough spit left to lick a postage stamp, I could scrape up enough to cool your kisser and make water cress sprout from it! (*Making an invocation.*) Kadidja! Kadidja! They say you're dead, since you're in the earth, but enter my body and inspire me! And as for Saïd, may he be blessed!

THE SOLDIER *leaves the brothel. Then* MALIKA *re-appears.*

MALIKA (*entering*): Their stiffness! It's gone into their gaze. . . . (*Noticing* WARDA's *golden rags.*) Say . . . looks as if there's been an explosion!

WARDA: Maybe they'll take me the way one picks a thistle: very carefully. Since they fuck us as if we were women . . .

Enter an Arab soldier. He makes a sign, then goes behind the screen.
WARDA *follows him.* MALIKA *is about to take up her sewing, but as*
HAMED *speaks, she remains attentive.*

HAMED (*to* OMMU): It's wrong of you to lose your temper.
We put up with you because women's insults are our
"Marseillaise," but there are times . . .

NEDJMA (*who has just entered*): Manure and insults are necessary.
You ought to be glad we women manure your courage
the way one manures squash.

BACHIR: One has to face reality. If something finally does
win out, what'll it be? Our corpse. And our corpses'll
fuck yours and your corpses'll give birth to little
corpses. . . .

ALL THE WOMEN: Boo! Boo! Boo! Boo! And you claimed
you were made of steel! of duralumin!

BACHIR: I may not be made of duralumin, but I remind you
that I'm one of the first and fiercest fighters. It was I
who set fire to the Nanteuils' farm, who butchered the
Bou Medina policeman, who rubbed out the two blue-eyed
soldiers. Well and good. But living in actual swinishness,
in filthiness, in shittiness, no! Putting arsenic in wells is a
sin.

OMMU: Do sins scare you? We've nothing else to live but sins,
we've got to live them. I have nothing against God, but
he can see that all he's left us is sins. And what's meant
by going into mourning, gentlemen, if not to make
oneself ugly? To cover oneself with crape, with ashes,
with mud, with flies, with cow dung, to let one's beard
grow, to let filth accumulate in the folds of the skin,
to pluck out one's eyes, to scrape one's fingers, what's
meant by going into mourning, gentlemen? (*Fervently.*)
Blessèd be Saïd!

NEDJMA: You'll die of thirst? So will we. But so will they.
And if they come back with their phonographs and
toilet water, I want the stench of my rotting carcass to
choke them to death.

OMMU (*to* BACHIR): For a thousand years we women have put up with being your dish rags, well and good, but for a hundred years *you've* been dish rags: thanks to you, the boots of those gentlemen have been a hundred thousand shining suns outshining the sun!

HAMED (*pointing to the ruins*): You can see what's become of us. . . .

HABIBA (*twenty years old; she has just entered*): We'll become worse. I'll do anything. I'm willing to catch your clap so I can pass it to the soldiers. (*She turns to the brothel, leans forward and yells.*) You'll teach me, Warda.

MALIKA (*very humbly*): They have everything, poor child: permanganate, gumma, methylene blue. . . . They're well protected. They have everything: hypodermic needles, capsules, adhesive tape.

THE SOLDIER *emerges from behind the screen, but instead of leaving the stage, he mounts the stairs and is thus at the watering trough. He looks at everyone but says nothing.*

SALEM: All right. It's *they* who'll be screwed, since all they'll find is a dead country. But we, we'll be washed up! And when we catch that Saïd of yours, he'll get what's coming to him!

OMMU: You shut up. (*Standing back as if to admire him.*) You're the handsomest and dumbest, that's a known fact. Content yourself with making gestures, striking poses, sticking out your tongue a little, fluttering your eyelashes and twitching your thighs. That'll soothe our eyes and the discussion can continue.

THE SOLDIER (*severely*): You shouldn't talk that way any more. And to speak of a traitor the way you do is wrong. And what else? A thief, a bastard, a beggar . . .

OMMU (*she is flabbergasted for a moment, then looks at* THE SOLDIER *ironically*):Aha!. . .that was to be expected! Because you boys have now reached the stage of uniforms, discipline, jaunty marches and bare arms, parade and heroic death, while singing "Madelon" and the "Marseillaise" and martial beauty. . . .

THE SOLDIER: Why not? There are other things than shit and filth. . . .

OMMU: You lousy little stinker, you snotnose, go join the other side where there's stately beauty, you little snotnose! But maybe you've done it, you're joining them, and copying them excites you. To be their reflection is already to be one of them: forehead to forehead, nose to nose, chin to chin, belly to belly, and why not, good God, why not make love with them, mouth to mouth, breath to breath, tongue to tongue, groan to groan, cry to cry. . . .

THE SOLDIER (*going toward* OMMU *with hostility, as she steps back*): Filth!

OMMU (*as with a cry of victory*): Aah! I've struck home, have I? War, love-making! Go ask those ladies of the whorehouse whether the warriors who come to their place . . . (*Addressing the brothel*): Hey! . . . Malika? Answer . . . Well, well, she's closed the window!

Suddenly a rumble of thunder. It is probably raining, since, with the exception of OMMU *and* SALEM, *half of the characters go to the right and the other half to the left, near the wings, and stand the way people stand under a shed to keep from getting wet.* OMMU *is alone, center, and she laughs.*

OMMU: But what could the water from the sky possibly wet? You're as thick as wires, not a drop could ever fall on you! (*She laughs.* SALEM *has come near her.*) Except you, Mr. Salem. You still here? It's true you're missing an arm, it must have melted in the rain.

SALEM (*he has gone to the bicycle, with a pump in his hand*): It melted in the fire of an ammunition dump. That entitles me to say what I think.

WARDA *reappears. She looks furious.*

WARDA (*to* MALIKA): Listen to them! Their passion! What *I* wanted to be was a whore, even in death. (*Angrily.*) Just listen to them! (*They listen.*)

OMMU: When the war's over, you'll be a veteran. For the time being, you've got a medical discharge. The war must be carried on. With hue and cry. And it's not from your mouth that eloquence flows but from your empty sleeve. Who's going to blow up your tires? Let me have it. (*She takes the bicycle pump from his hand, removes a valve from the front wheel and starts blowing up the tire. Between her teeth.*) Blowing you up! . . . Always having to puff you up!

THE SOLDIER (*approaching*): *We're* burning with anger too, but our anger is slower. We have to carry the machine gun and set it up. Have to feed it. Have to watch the horizon. A rebellion's taking place, but *our* rebellion is weightier. You can dance all around us and sing, but we have to protect your dances, your waltzes, and your insults. (*He tries to take the pump, but* OMMU *refuses to let go of it.*)

SALEM (*to* OMMU): And even your abuse is going to dry up. The flow's becoming weaker and weaker.

OMMU (*raising her head*): Am I getting old?

THE SOLDIER (*sadly*): I'll be dead before you, so I'm the elder.

OMMU (*straightening her back and looking* THE SOLDIER *in the eyes*): I know your worth. All of you. (*She is grave.*) I

know that Death has his eye on you. These days, he
carries off our youngest first, but he's making you play
a dangerous game. In the past, you were unripe fruit
that fell from the tree on a stormy night. Now . . .

THE SOLDIER (*sharply*): War teaches us what peace will be.
Neither killing nor getting killed, no, we want to be
the stronger. We need armor.

OMMU (*arrogantly*): To protect what?

THE SOLDIER (*after a pause*): I have no idea. But we need it.
Hurry up and blow up his tires. I don't want to stand in
the rain.

OMMU (*ironically*): You're worrying about your nice uniform. . . .

THE SOLDIER (*moving off and going to protect himself*): That too.
One fights less well in rags. (*With sudden venom.*) And
one fights less well when one has an ugly mug and is
less attractive to women. (*In a fury.*) And if men are to
envy our death, then our way of going out to die must
make them envious! . . .

OMMU (*she shrugs and starts pumping again*): Kadidja . . .

SALEM: Don't bother . . . We'll be drenched, don't bother
about the bike. (*He takes it by the handlebars.*)

OMMU: You're right. I'll certainly be coughing in the morning,
I have very delicate vocal cords. (*She replaces the pump
on the frame of the bicycle.*) I know very well he's right. . . .
(*She points to* THE SOLDIER.) But Kadidja said what had
to be said.

*Below, in the brothel, a soldier enters. He goes behind the screen,
where* MALIKA *follows him.* WARDA *looks more and more furious.*

MALIKA (*before disappearing*): If he crashes down on me, I'll
come back drenched!

SALEM (*leaving with his bicycle under his arm*): Don't forget that
she said it when she was dead. She wouldn't have dared

to when she was alive. (OMMU *hesitates to reply.*) Hurry up,
I'm getting wet.

THE SOLDIER (*crying out*): To protect what? Armor to protect
what? Why, simply your bullshit, old girl! Simply that.
Seeing you just made me realize it. If we die, I agree,
it's not for that, but if we organize with law and order,
it's so that you can live a hundred years with your sweet
. . . your sweet . . . your tender, luminous bullshit. . . .

OMMU (*ironically*): So it's as precious as all that? (*With sudden
anxiety.*) What about Saïd? Anyone know anything about
Saïd? (*She coughs.*)

*They manage to take shelter, shivering, waiting for the rain to stop,
until the end of the scene.*

THE SOLDIER (*who has just taken shelter*): I'd be the one to know,
before anyone else. I've been ordered to bring him
back to the commanding officer dead or alive. To find
him . . .

OMMU (*laughing*): Like a hunting dog the quail! But you first
have to find him, to scent him, to sniff about, and you
don't have a sense of smell. It's up to us to find Saïd
and preserve him, to bottle him.

THE SOLDIER: If I want to sniff about . . .

OMMU: Saïd's for us.

The rear screen moves aside. SAÏD *appears, motionless, smiling and
self-possessed. He has his thumbs in his belt and his hands flat against
his thighs. He moves his shoulders casually.*

SAÏD (*without moving*): No, Admiral. No, don't offer me your
fingers with tongs, don't put on gloves, I've no desire
to move my mitts. The big job's been done. I've let you
know where to direct your boats in order to cut off your

enemy's retreat. The channel? What channel? Your
boats? Your cruisers? It's not my business to know if
boats can climb mountains. I've followed instructions.
It's you who are at the helm. . . .

The screen moves back, concealing SAÏD. *Nobody appears to have
heard him. Everyone seems to be protecting himself from the rain.*

WARDA (*looking at herself again*): Mirror, mirror, where is
the time when I could stare at myself, and yawn, for
hours on end? (*She spits on the mirror.*) Where are the men
who used to stare at me staring at myself without daring
to breathe? Now we plug away. And answering hello
to the women who greet you at the grocer's is less restful
than I'd have thought. . . .

The Arab soldier leaves, combing his hair. MALIKA *reappears, tying
her belt.*

MALIKA: He was covered with blood. . . . I'm going to sew
some hooks on my belt. (*She sews.*)
WARDA: Your vivacity predestined you to become a sewing
machine. There was a great distance, there was a Sahara
Desert, between me, Warda, and the most despised
woman of the village, between me and Leila. A major
in the Colonial Artillery—I'm speaking of a year ago—
turned up one afternoon, three of his buttons were loose:
it was he, with his fat ringed fingers, who sewed them
on his fly, I didn't know how to. Now I do. Suck the
thread, thread the needle, put on a patch, cut on the bias
. . . At the butcher's, at the grocer's, they say hello
to me . . . I'm less and less someone . . . and my anger
is greater and greater, and so is my sadness. But they'd
better beware of my sadness. It's my sadness that's going

to make me invent the misfortune that's been taken away from me. . . .

MALIKA (*gently*): Please, Warda, be calm. (*She goes up to* WARDA, *with an air of tenderness.*)

WARDA (*screaming*): A nurse! . . . A nurse! . . . They drag me from my grave in order to make me a lady of the Red Cross. (*Facing* OMMU.) Round about me, with my hands, I built the whorehouse. Stone by stone, you're demolishing it in order to get at my heart. . . .

THE SOLDIER (*with a movement of manly boasting*): As long as there are soldiers there'll be whores.

DJEMILA *enters at this moment, right. She is carrying a small black valise. Above, all the men are interested in her arrival.*

WARDA: Who are you?

DJEMILA: My name's Djemila and I've arrived from Mainz.

MALIKA: Are you a good worker?

DJEMILA (*putting down her valise*): Mainz, garrison town. In addition to a well-stacked corset, I have a strong back. And a springy one—it's been pounded on a bed harder than a church pew, by English soldiers, American soldiers, German, Russian, Polish, Senegalese . . . (*She looks at* WARDA'*s rags.*) Are they fighting here right up to the whorehouse?

WARDA (*raging*): They're screwing here, in the cathouse.

Above, left, THE CADI *enters. He is about to leave by the rear, but* OMMU *stops him.*

OMMU: Well, Cadi? In the rain! It'll be beautiful, that ever-so-beautiful justice that you made so beautiful.

THE CADI (*laughing*): If I made it so beautiful for you, you can go fuck it. Do as you like with it. . . .

OMMU: It's yours. . . .

THE CADI (*laughing*): No longer mine. Things cease to belong to those who've been able to make them more beautiful. Once they've been freed, delivered, they scoot off and go live elsewhere, on whom, on what, how they live, I don't give a shit, I don't give a fuck. (*The women burst out laughing.*) . . . better and more beautiful, light-footed, wingèd, they gratefully abandon the one who made them better. When they've gone, nothing left, not a particle, zero, pfft! (*He laughs.*)

At this moment, the whistling of a march is heard in the distance, as if coming from the countryside. The characters around the watering trough and those from the brothel raise their heads as if to look into the distance, high up.

DJEMILA: What is it?

MALIKA (*sadly*): Our boys. Our fighters. They're coming down the side of the hill . . . nothing stops them, neither the mud on their boots nor the rain on their hats. . . . (*She listens.*) It's evening already and they're returning to quarters . . . dog-tired. . . .

THE SOLDIER (*joyfully*): There they are!

MALIKA: All day long they've been killing, slashing, butchering. . . .

DJEMILA: And they whistle?

NEDJMA and OMMU: There they are!

MALIKA (*to* DJEMILA): Yes, it didn't take them long to learn. There must be a phonograph in each platoon that plays the same tune all day and all night.

DJEMILA: Perhaps before long, if they whistle so well and march with a wiggle of the ass, like the Americans, perhaps we . . .

ALL THE CHARACTERS UP ABOVE (*together*): There they are!

Listen! They're marching in quick time! They've got a military band! . . . They kill with machine guns. . . . They have a flag. . . .

WARDA (*screaming*): No! No! Not me! I'll never float, never will I be beaten by the wind!

OMMU: And before launching an attack, I hope they drink wine, as is forbidden by the Koran. Once they sin against the Book, they can dare anything! Take it, Saïd!

Above, at the watering trough, everyone goes behind the two screens. Below, too, the whores conceal themselves, But above, the rear screen moves slightly to the side, as before, revealing SAÏD, *who is still motionless.*

SAÏD (*who is alone on the stage*): Done, Leila! With the eye you've got left, if you can see me, I'm relaxed, Leila. With my thumbs in my belt and my hands flat on my thighs, the way they do it in America. And don't worry about a thing, I've shot the works. It's going to be hard making a getaway with all those snouts on my tracks. And I stink as much as you. I hope I've shown the right way. Though at bottom all ways are alike. Leila . . . (*He yells.*) Leila! . . . if you see steamboats crossing the rye fields, if you see sailors in the alfalfa . . .

SCENE FIFTEEN

On the floor, a series of transparent, white paper screens arranged one behind the other at intervals of about three feet. In two quarter circles, right and left, several Arabs, men and women. Among them: SI SLIMANE, NEDJMA, BRAHIM *and* MUSTAPHA, *and* PIERRE, *the French Soldier. Left, a paper screen, behind which we see the silhouette of a woman who is hesitating. Above: another screen, in front of which will appear* THE MOTHER, *then* THE LIEUTENANT *and the soldiers.*

The Arabs all break into very soft laughter. Finally, the woman who was hesitating behind the screen, left, breaks through the paper of the screen: it is KADIDJA. *She seems very much at ease and breaks into the same soft laughter.*

KADIDJA (*she stops laughing and wipes her eyes*): Well, well! (*She laughs again.*)

SI SLIMANE (*laughing softly*): That's right!

KADIDJA (*laughing again*): Well what do you know!

SI SLIMANE (*approvingly*): That's it!

KADIDJA (*looking about her*): And they make such a fuss about it!

SI SLIMANE: Why not? Got to have a little fun.

KADIDJA (*laughing less and less*): True enough . . . but all the same . . . who'd have thought it? (*Suddenly anxious.*) Tell me, did it take me long to get here?

SI SLIMANE: You were killed at 3:24 A.M., their time, up above, down there, and here you are, three days later.

KADIDJA (*smiling*): What's one supposed to do?

NEDJMA: Nothing. Nothing to do. Usually, time passes, like coffee through a strainer, and in the strainer it filters the inessential. Now time no longer passes.

KADIDJA: What does it do?

SI SLIMANE: Time does nothing either.

KADIDJA: Does it get bored?

SI SLIMANE: When questioned, it doesn't speak.

KADIDJA: Therefore, I don't speak.

SI SLIMANE: You stammer. You still have some bits of time flowing between your teeth.

KADIDJA: You people don't seem to realize what I did for them down there. I organized the rebellion, drew the men into it, and died for freedom.

BRAHIM: The fact is we couldn't care less. Everybody dies in one way or another. Me, for example, I died in a mine in Belgium.

KADIDJA (*noting the fact, dismally*): In Belgium.

BRAHIM (*pointing to* MUSTAPHA): And he, he was a diver at the Cherbourg shipyard.

KADIDJA: All dead, very well, but are you all Moslems?

BRAHIM (*smiling*): For the time being, so that we feel at home. Afterwards . . .

KADIDJA: After what? There's no more afterwards if there's no more time.

SI SLIMANE (*smiling*): No more time, but something else, as mysterious to us as time to the living.

Each of the characters seems to be musing.

KADIDJA: But then, if we're among ourselves, do we carry on the fight? We can still help those up above?

SI SLIMANE: Help them become what we wanted to become when we were up there?

KADIDJA: Yes.

They all burst into very soft laughter.

BRAHIM: That would mean trying to die less. And one must die more and more.

KADIDJA: All the same, a part of me's still back there.

SI SLIMANE: What?

KADIDJA: The image of me that I left behind . . . Can I see it?

SI SLIMANE: Do you want to know whether they've found out that for twenty years you sold yourself to soldiers? Everyone knew it by the end of the first month.

Suddenly the screen above lights up slightly. It is all black, with nothing on it. THE MOTHER *appears, dragging the dead soldier by the belt. All the dead lower their heads (although* THE MOTHER *is above them) in order to look at her. Thus, the corpse of* PIERRE *appears below, dragged by the straps.*

THE MOTHER (*grumbling*): . . . and of the ocean! . . . Kings of the world and of the ocean . . . (*She is out of breath.*) . . . Of rubies, you drag beneath your crowns of rubies, a load of refuse. . . .

KADIDJA (*looking down*): It's Saïd's mother, Leila's mother-in-law!

SI SLIMANE: We've been observing her for some time now, but all she does is one damn fool thing after the other. She who's usually so intelligent, one would think she was dying against the grain, and without rhyme or reason.

THE MOTHER (*still dragging the corpse*): Oh, oh, I'm getting wet! Just because I said a few words about the ocean, here am I all soaked! . . . The gods are tough. But when they realize what I'm made of, they'll think it over. . . .

The corpse of PIERRE, *that is, the actor who is playing* PIERRE, *stands up slowly, smiling.*

KADIDJA: Where is she at the present moment?

SI SLIMANE: Nowhere. But not yet quite nowhere. She'll be there shortly, when she's with us. . . .

PIERRE: Well, well!

KADIDJA (*pointing to* PIERRE): That's right! But . . . but him, there, he's the one she's dragging!

PIERRE: She couldn't follow. . . . She's firmly planted on earth, the bitch. . . . But me, I hotfooted it here. . . .

KADIDJA (*seeming to take no further interest in what is happening*): Sulmerge. . . . Sulmerge. . . . Here! There! On my . . . here, on my finger . . . no, not on the joint . . . not you! Ephebas! . . . Errima! . . . (*She seems amazed, looks at* THE SOLDIER, *who is as surprised as she, and they laugh together.*)

PIERRE (*admiringly*): Made it!

KADIDJA: And it seemed easy to me! . . . As clear as the relationship between space and running.

THE MOTHER (*she is about to leave the stage*): Go away! . . . (*She implores.*) Your Excellencies the gods, go away! . . . Go away! . . . Let me extricate myself from the thorns, the belts, the corpses . . . the living . . . the loving . . . the laughing . . . the fish, the lakes and the oceans! . . . I'm a thoroughbred bitch that fishes and hunts. (*Exit* THE MOTHER.)

KADIDJA (*looking at* SI SLIMANE): She off her nut?

SI SLIMANE (*smiling*): Like you a while ago . . . she's going through the forest. . . . She's peeling off reason so as to arrive pure and like you to know the relationships between space and running, and the names of flies.

KADIDJA (*calling out*): Ephebas! . . . Ernimont! . . . Sulmerge! . . . Holgane! . . . Cebelladone! . . . Nictuel! . . . Emelogue! . . . Catalogue! . . . Sarfesse, Crapesse!

SI SLIMANE: Whom are you calling, the dead flies or the live ones?

But KADIDJA *does not answer. From the rear of the stage, behind the many paper screens, appears a tiny silhouette. It slowly goes through all the screens, ripping them; it grows bigger and bigger as it draws near. Finally, it is behind the last screen, that is, the one nearest the audience, and, tearing this last sheet of paper, appears: it is* THE MOTHER.

THE MOTHER (*laughing softly*): Well, well!

PIERRE (*laughing softly*): That's right!

THE MOTHER: Well what do you know!

PIERRE: That's it!

Everyone laughs.

THE MOTHER: And they make such a fuss about it!

PIERRE: Why not? Got to have a little fun.

THE MOTHER: True enough . . . but all the same . . . who'd have thought it? So I'm dead? (*To* KADIDJA): It's you, Kadidja.

All the others leave quietly, except PIERRE.

KADIDJA (*smiling*): I died first.

THE MOTHER: Where does it get you?

KADIDJA (*smiling*): Look. (*She calls out.*) Sulmerge! . . . Ephebas!
. . . Mentriloque! . . . Salgaz! . . . Vri . . . Mri . . . Sri! . . .

THE MOTHER (*astounded*): You know them all! You learn fast.
You've been blessed with a good memory.

KADIDJA: What about you, how'd you manage to kick off
so soon? Are you running after me?

THE MOTHER: It would seem so, but not exactly that. I died
of exhaustion.

KADIDJA (*laughing*): But before you did you made it your
business to kill one of them.

THE MOTHER (*pretending to be shocked*): Me? . . . Not at all!
(*She looks at* PIERRE.) Him? His neck got caught in the
straps.

PIERRE (*laughing*): You did your best to twist me up. And you
kept pulling . . . and pulling!

THE MOTHER (*to* KADIDJA, *who is roaring with laughter*): Yet I
arranged it all so it would be by accident.

KADIDJA (*smiling*): But why? You always hated us all. And
the feeling was mutual! (*She bursts out laughing and* THE
MOTHER *does likewise.*) What a beating you took, you
and Saïd and Leila! And slobbering! And shitting!
And belching! And pissing fire! Puking your guts
out! . . .

THE MOTHER (*laughing*): And wallowing in shit up to our
lips! And watch out for the splashing, the waves, clench
your teeth! (*She laughs harder.*)

KADIDJA: It's because of that?

THE MOTHER: It's because of that. (*Smiling.*) In every village,
my beloved Kadidja, there's a little plot of ground that
stinks, called the public dump. That's where all the
filth from the local garbage cans is piled up. Every
dump has its smell and it's not the same in Grenoble
as in Upsala, Sweden. It's a long time since the blood

stopped flowing from my thirteen holes—knives, bayonets and bullets—but the smell of our garbage cans is still in my nostrils . . . (*She takes a breath and speaks more loudly.*) . . . the smell I smelled all my life, and that's what I'll be composed of here when I'm completely dead, and I have every hope of polluting death too. . . . I want it to be my rot that rots my village. . . .

KADIDJA (*laughing too*): With me, it's my flies! I have billions and billions of them, but it's as if they all added up to less than one, as if they added up to only two! I send them out to lay their eggs on the eyelids of four-year-old beggars, in the bellies of our slaughtered cows, and to buzz about the corpses of our soldiers. Watch out!

All heads are lowered while the upper screen lights up again.

SI SLIMANE (*softly*): It's autumn . . . it's autumn. . . .
THE MOTHER (*surprised*): Is it some of them following me? . . .

Four members of the Foreign Legion appear, bent under their packs, walking slowly in the darkness. Their mud-stained uniforms are in rags. The actors will speak in a muffled tone, as whenever they play the role of soldiers. The dead will look down, although the scene they are watching is played above.

ROGER (*he looks very weary; he walks toward the right wing*): You're suspicious of every stone! Watch your step, the ravine's at the left. . . .
NESTOR (*appearing; he is exhausted*): The enemy is everything that moves and everything that doesn't move. He's the water that moves and the water that doesn't move, and he's the wind that we inhale.
ROGER (*farting, and in a grave voice*): Inhale mine, it's wind from Gascony.

NESTOR (*holding his nose*): Re-pul-sive!

During the entire scene, even when THE LIEUTENANT *is on stage, the actors are to speak as if they do not see each other. Their gaze never meets that of the person they are addressing. They are to give the impression of being in pitch darkness.*

ROGER (*taking off his shoes, which no longer have soles*): My soles are gone, and I'm walking on the skin of my feet. So it's not to the soles of my feet that our country's attached, it's deposited in my belly. In order to be surrounded by it, I leave a fart. If all the boys from the Pyrenees do the same, and those from Toulouse and from Bordeaux, et cetera, we'll be able to say we're fighting in the air of Guyenne and Gascony. (*Stopping suddenly and turning around.*) Shall we wait for him?

NESTOR: Is someone traveling?

ROGER: You know who I'm talking about.

NESTOR (*bumping into* ROGER): Let him follow. He's practically being carried in a sedan chair. He's already excused from carrying a pack and feels free to go strolling about and piss in the flowers.

ROGER (*stopping*): Treats himself to the luxury of choosing the ones that receive his dew drops. . . . We can walk a little slower. . . .

NESTOR (*trying to pass*): He won't lose his way in the darkness; he's luminous. He shines with the luster of his exploits.

ROGER: Jealous? . . . Watch your step, I told you, or we'll go rolling down. (*They make careful gestures, as if they were on a very narrow and dangerous path.*) Not jealous? *I* am, at times. I envy his coolness. . . . Goddamn it, don't push! . . .

NESTOR (*shivering*): He freezes me from a distance. And his mug is frozen.

JOJO (*spitefully*): *He's* the one who wears his mug. And before long, we may have one just like it. All of us.

THE LIEUTENANT (*appearing, left*): Keep going. . . . Be careful, but keep going.

ROGER: He's far behind, Sir. . . .

THE LIEUTENANT: Don't worry, he'll join us. . . . (*Bitterly.*) *He's* not limping. He's steady on his feet. . . .

ROGER (*roughly*): Sir . . .

THE LIEUTENANT (*curtly, advancing slightly, with a limp*): Keep going. (*Then, in a gentler tone.*) What can we do with him? We're about to enter death. If we get out of it, it'll be by the skin of our teeth. As for him, his cruelty consumes him and makes him gleam: we may be spotted because of him. And if, by any chance, we're saved, what'll we do with him? And he, what'll he do with himself? I saw him, without his being aware. I hid behind a bush and watched him. When he's alone, he sees only himself. . . . (*A pause. All of them, very gently, make the gestures of blind people without touching anything.*) . . . I'm going to investigate. (*He bends forward, groping his way. He lies down and puts his ear to the ground. He listens. Then, he raises himself slightly.*) He's coming. With my ear on the path, I can hear him coming, very quickly, with noiseless steps, with long, sure strides. . . . (*He gets to his feet.*) Be careful not to send the stones rolling down the ravine. . . . Keep going! . . . The darkness protects *him*, but not us. . . . There's probably a mass of rock at the end of the path. . . . Go around it quietly. . . . You don't want him to join us either. . . .

Suddenly a shot. THE LIEUTENANT *collapses. He is now going to speak very quickly, and in a low voice. The three soldiers, then a fourth,* ROLAND, *who has just entered, turn to him. They make groping gestures, which indicate that the scene is taking place in the darkness.*

THE LIEUTENANT: That does it, lads. The bullet's come. And I'm dying gropingly. . . . I haven't much left. . . . Our country's far away. . . . I was worthy of a general's stars, yet I won't even have received a lieutenant-colonel's bars. . . . Water . . . (THE LIEUTENANT *remains lying on his belly.*)

JOJO (*gently*): There's none left, Sir.

THE LIEUTENANT: Water . . .

ROLAND: He's going to kick off.

NESTOR: There's nothing we can do for him. We'll wait till he passes out, then close his eyes and toss him into the ravine.

JOJO (*in a very gentle voice*): But first let's give him something to drink.

ROGER: What, a bowl of air?

JOJO: If that's all we've got, let's give it ungrudgingly. Of course . . . (*He hesitates.*) . . . he won't be on French soil, but even so we can . . .

NESTOR: Leave a fart, that's easy to say, but what about those whose bellies aren't bloated?

ROGER: They should've thought of that before. When I left home, I filled up with local air. I unpleat my asshole and my country surrounds me.

JOJO (*very gently*): Since that's all we've got . . . the Lieutenant'll have the illusion of dying on home soil. (*He hesitates.*) Nestor, if you've got any spare gas, and the others too . . . we could shoot him a whiff of it. . . .

NESTOR: All I've got left is my ration.

ROLAND: The trouble with me is that every time I open a crack to get a whiff of the town hall, bango, there's a draft and there's no telling who gets the benefit of it.

THE LIEUTENANT (*in a dying voice*): Water . . .

They all look at him, then turn away.

JOJO: If he's not buried in Christian soil, at least let him die breathing some air from home. . . .

NESTOR: Nothing. That's all I had left, a few bubbles popping in the coils of my guts. What'll I have left afterwards? A flat belly. Flat! Because I know what generosity and magnificence are. If we all pitch in, we'll be giving him an official funeral. There'll be an aroma of Gascony within a radius of five miles.

ROLAND: Maybe he has what's needed inside himself. Let him make an effort. . . .

JOJO: Got to be human. You can't ask a dying man . . . (*A pause.*)

ROGER (*with a gesture of rage*): All right, I get you. Turn him over.

THE LIEUTENANT: Water . . .

The soldiers turn THE LIEUTENANT *over and lean him against the screen.*

ROGER: Put him down gently, with his back against the rock. And do your job silently. The enemy's in the neighborhood but, thanks to us, in the hostile darkness and countryside there'll be a Christian death chamber with the smell of candles, wreaths, a last will and testament, a death chamber set up there like a cloud in a painting. . . . Get set, boys. (*To* THE LIEUTENANT): Sir, you won't go down among the dead without harmony and a little local air. (*To* NESTOR): You who know music, stand over there. But soft-pedal it. The dying man's a delicate chap and the place isn't safe. (NESTOR *faces the audience. To* THE LIEUTENANT): Sir, open your ears and nostrils. . . . Fire!

ROGER *himself goes and places his ass above* THE LIEUTENANT'*s face.* NESTOR *slaps his own face with his finger and makes a farting sound.*

ROGER: That's Gascony.

He makes way for JOJO, *who assumes the stance of a pissing dog, with a leg raised above* THE LIEUTENANT, *and leaves his fart, but the sound is made by* NESTOR *with his hand under his arm.*

JOJO: That's a refrain from Lorraine.

He makes way for ROLAND, *who squats, then squeezes, but the sound is again made by* NESTOR, *this time with his hand against his mouth.*

ROLAND: Greetings from Normandy.

NESTOR *leaves his place and goes to fart on* THE LIEUTENANT. *He forces himself, but nothing comes. He takes the scarf he was wearing around his neck and rips it from top to bottom.*

NESTOR: Brittany delegation.
ROGER (*gravely*): Thanks, boys, he's had his official funeral and the enemy hasn't spotted us.
ROLAND: About the rocks lingers the odor . . .
ROGER: Lift him gently. (*The soldiers take* THE LIEUTENANT *and carry him behind the screen.*) And send the stuff tumbling from ravine to ravine.

Exit ROGER, *too, behind the screen.*

THE MOTHER (*smiling*): Does that mean he's coming?
KADIDJA (*same smile*): Won't be long now. And the others, too. But there's more to it than that. . . . (*Laughing harder.*) . . . there're my flies. You know that I'm a kind of sultana of flies here, or, if you prefer, an official delegate of the flies!
THE MOTHER (*astounded*): Will you send a battalion or two of them to my dump?

KADIDJA (*laughing*): Right away . . . (*She makes a gesture, as if calling.*)

THE MOTHER (*laughing*): We have time. Let's chat a bit. What do you think they're going to do, down there?

KADIDJA (*laughing*): Nothing, poor wretches. Too much was expected of them. Where does it get you, plunging into muck?

THE MOTHER (*laughing, and* KADIDJA *with her*): Nowhere, I realize that, but that's why! (*She roars with laughter, and it is with roars of laughter that she says the following.*) Those are the truths . . . ha! . . . ha! . . . ha! ha! . . . that can't be demonstrated . . . ha! ha! (*Her laughter seems uncontrollable.*) Those are the truths that are false! . . . ha! ha! ha! ho! ho! ho! . . . ha! ha! . . . (*She is bent double with laughter.*) Those are the truths you can't carry to their extremes . . . ho! ho! ho! ho! Oh! oh! Ha! ha! Ho! ho! ho! . . . without seeing them die and without seeing yourself die of laughter, that you've got to exalt, it's those, to the point of death! ha! ha! ha! ho! ho! ho! ho! ha! ha!

KADIDJA (*laughing harder then* THE MOTHER): No one'll ever be able to apply them! Ha! ha! ha! ha!

THE MOTHER (*rolling on the ground with laughter*): Never! . . . Never! . . . They've got to . . . th . . . th . . . ey . . . they've got to ha! ha! ha! ha! ho! ho! ho! ho! . . . they've got to sing and give headaches.

They writhe on the ground with laughter until they have hiccups.

KADIDJA: And when I saw you you didn't see! ha! ha! Talking crap like no technician ever, talking crap hearing you . . . ha! ha! ha! ho! ho! ho! . . . talking to the thorns about your man and how handsome he was, the beggar . . . ha! ha! . . .

THE MOTHER (*laughing as hard as* KADIDJA): And me even saying

that . . . ha! ha! ha! ho! ho! that he was so handsome that
when I saw him I started snoozing . . . snoring . . . ha!
ha! ha! And that Saïd . . . Saïd, like my left shoe that I
found broken in a garbage can! . . . (*Suddenly she seems to
come to her senses.*) Saïd? Saïd, no, but Leila? What's
become of Leila? Where's she gone?

*The whole stage grows dark. The screens disappear into the wings. A
moment of waiting. Silence. Then* LEILA *appears, left. She is wearing
high-heeled shoes. She will speak very soberly, without seeking effect.
She will remain motionless throughout the speech.*

LEILA: If I could at least pick up my eye and put it back. Or
find another one, a blue one, or a pink one! But mine's
lost. (*A pause.*) Go away. (*She makes a gesture of driving
someone away.*) Go away, stink! . . . Who told you to stand
beside me? . . . Oh well, sit down there if you like, and
don't move, sovereign. (*A pause.*) Saïd, my nice Saïd, you
put my eye out and you did right. Two eyes, that was a
bit too much . . . as for the rest, yes I know, I've got the itch
and my thighs are full of scabs. (*She drives away the flies.*)
Go away, ladies. You'll be back in an hour, on my
corpse. . . . Saïd, I understand your leaving me. . . .
You're expected at the turning for a greater destiny, and
you knew it. You were getting conceited, unbearable.
Conceited as a schoolteacher . . . He's looking for me,
when he finds me I'll be stiff. Cold, chapped, emptied,
wrinkled, a kind of little dick on a frosty night. . . . (*She
laughs.*) Poor Saïd! (*She listens attentively.*) Keep yelling.
That's all part of the story. As for me, I'm going to stretch
out and kick off. . . . Keep yelling. I know you delivered
the goods. You were way ahead of me in rattiness, but all
the same I'm the wife of a traitor. And that deserves
consideration and an empress's couch. (*She listens attentively.*)

Is that you yelling, Saïd? Keep yelling. If you found me you'd be obliged to take care of me, to save me . . . and now, with only one eye, I'm going to have to descend to death. (*A pause.*) I wonder how to go about it. Because the question is: is death a lady, like the smell I told to sit down beside me on the manure pile—are you there?—a lady who'll come and get me, or is it a place you have to go to? Hard to tell . . . (*A long silence. Then, the hooting of an owl.*) Yes . . . that's right. . . . What? . . . What? Which way? . . . Yes . . . yes, don't be too rough . . . yes. There . . . there where there's light? All right. (*A cry.*) Oh! Damn it, I'm rising! I'm floating to the surf . . . No? . . . no? I'm going down you think. . . . (*She starts backing upstage.*) You see . . . I'm rising . . . a lurch . . . it's the hollow . . . of a wave of time. . . . Oh, nothing more. Is it the bottom? . . . I'm rising . . . and I'm floating up to the surf . . . No? No. All right, if you say so that means it's true since everything's starting to be true . . . all right. . . . There. Let's sink again with both shoulders. . . . (*She disappears.*)

SCENE SIXTEEN

The screens are set up on two levels. Above, again the many white screens that the dead will traverse. Below, on the floor of the stage, toward the left, an unlighted screen. This will be the brothel.

Six women, visible in spite of the slight darkness on this level of the stage, are sitting about the corpse of a woman and knitting in silence. All the dead men and women (they are all Arabs) are in the throes of the same fit of trembling, except SI SLIMANE.

BRAHIM (*with terror*): They're going to come . . . they're coming!

SI SLIMANE (*smiling*): You resemble warped wheels. . . .

BRAHIM: All I brought with me from life, all I have left from life, is my trembling. If it's taken away from me, I lose everything, I'm no longer anything.

SI SLIMANE (*still smiling*): Were the shakes all you had in life? . . . or maybe you didn't have enough of them. . . . Don't be afraid of the dead, they're dead.

KADIDJA: Not quite, since they get deader and deader.

SI SLIMANE: You know a lot more than they about the harm one can do in death. (*Thoughtfully.*) Yes, here one dies increasingly, but not as there. . . .

From very far off, visible behind the screens, shadows arrive. Then the shadows pierce the paper and go through it: they are the soldiers, guided by THE GENERAL. *After a short pause they cross the stage and stare, without seeing them, at the Arabs, who tremble and leave, left.*

THE GENERAL (*laughing*): Well, well!

THE ARABS (*together, without ceasing to tremble*): That's right!

THE GENERAL: Well what do you know! (*He walks by and leaves, left.*)

THE LIEUTENANT (*following* THE GENERAL, *and likewise laughing*): Well, well!

THE ARABS: That's right!

THE LIEUTENANT: Well what do you know!

THE ARABS (*smiling, but trembling*): That's it.

THE LIEUTENANT: And they make such a fuss about it! (*He laughs complacently.*) The hardest part of all . . . (*He laughs a little more loudly.*) . . . was getting away from my country that suddenly invaded me . . . (*He laughs again.*) . . . in fact, a bit of it's still clinging to the hairs in my nose. . . .

SI SLIMANE (*smiling*): Good thing it's no more than an odor clinging to the hairs in your nose.

THE LIEUTENANT *walks by and leaves, left.*

ROGER (*laughing*): Well, well!

THE ARABS: That's right.

ROGER: Well what do you know! (*He walks by and leaves.*)

PRESTON, NESTOR, RITON (*together and laughing*): Well, well!

THE ARABS: That's right!

PRESTON, NESTOR, RITON: Well what do you know!

They walk by and leave, left. Then come about a dozen soldiers who say the same thing and leave. THE ARABS *reply as above. A silence.* THE ARABS *stop trembling.*

THE MOTHER (*laughing*): Well what do you know!

KADIDJA: They didn't even try to hurt me. Yet they must know . . .

BRAHIM: I . . . in spite of my trembling, I looked at them, and I didn't recognize them. Really and truly, they looked gentle and . . . maybe . . . kind.

SI SLIMANE: They were becoming so . . . with astonishment.

KADIDJA: It's about time!

THE MOTHER (*laughing gently*): I'd like to know what's happening to her.

SI SLIMANE (*laughing*): She's sinking real slow. She's dying the way she lived: like a lazybones.

KADIDJA (*laughing*): The eye of the revolver has the serpent's gaze.

Suddenly THE SERGEANT *appears—dead, of course. His face is all white: it is smeared with grease paint, like the faces of the other dead, except for a long streak of very red blood from his forehead to his chin. His whole chest is covered with multicolored clanking decorations.*

THE SERGEANT (*laughing*): Well, well!

BRAHIM (*also laughing*): That's right!

THE SERGEANT: Well what do you know!

BRAHIM: That's it!

THE SERGEANT: And they make such a fuss about it!

BRAHIM: Why not?

THE SERGEANT (*laughing louder*): . . . and that it would be a stain on my death . . . (*He laughs.*) It was repeated to me often enough, and here I am laughing heartily like a hoyden! . . . A stain on my death. (*He laughs and all the dead laugh with him.*) I was rough in my ways, but God-damn it a male has what it takes for that . . . ha! ha! ha! (*He and all the other dead laugh harder and harder.*) . . . and damn it all, I honored the men. I, Sergeant Gadget, say that when they had the jitters, the shakes, when they were crapping in their pants . . . ha! ha! ho! ho! ho! crapping! ha! ha! ha! ha! ho! ho! ho! . . . crapping! ho! ho! . . . crapping in their pants, that the men lost what makes them vile . . . (*He and the dead writhe with laughter.*) . . . their eyes! . . . their eyes! . . . blue or black . . . their eyes in the throes of the jitters, the bastards, their eyes! . . . (*All laugh more and more loudly.*) . . . you could see it all in their eyes! . . . To say nothing of the fact that I was always followed in darkness and daylight by the one who was going ahead of me. (*He writhes with laughter and leaves. The other dead continue to laugh. They get over their fit gradually.*)

SI SLIMANE (*still laughing; with a shrug*): That's one way of looking

at things. (*A pause.*) My own image is already blurred.
. . . Time passes less and less. . . .

THE MOTHER (*laughing*): . . . she's going to sink to the bottom
for certain, the idiot. She was never able to make the
slightest move to help herself! But I'm talking about Saïd.
Who sees him?

SI SLIMANE: I don't have much time left for talking. I'm
dwindling . . . I'm melting . . . I'm melted. . . .

THE MOTHER (*laughing*): Saïd!

SI SLIMANE: He bungled his job . . . but don't get upset . . .
there's nothing lost. . . . He did what he could . . . when
he was caught . . . questioned . . . he told which path
our patrols had taken . . . but that day . . . I'm melting
. . . I've melt . . . (*He laughs.*)

THE MOTHER (*annoyed*): That day?

SI SLIMANE: In any case, he's dead. Shot point-blank by our
soldiers.

THE MOTHER: Died how?

SI SLIMANE: Oh please, let me vanish completely . . . I'm
melting . . . I've melted . . . (*He laughs.*)

*Suddenly a hammering is heard. The women seem to pay no attention
to it. They knit. Above, the dead are getting excited.*

KADIDJA: It's that cage. They're still nailing. They'll soon
be done.

THE MOTHER (*smiling*): I see very well how they're going to
finish off Warda. They'll leave blood with their knitting
needles. They're not very clever. (*Hammering again.*) Yet
the spectacle's worth a look: six knitters pounced on the
lady who'd managed to become the most artful whore in
the world. Together they were a giant hornet armed with
six rust-proof steel stings. I saw it all: the hornet swooped
down on the flower and pierced the skin of its belly and

neck . . . the blood spurting and spotting them, and the poor thing straining every muscle to breathe her last. . . . (*A pause; then, smiling slightly.*) And Leila still hasn't come! Something ought to be done to help her. . . . (*A pause.*)

KADIDJA: Don't be impatient. I know her, she always did things in her own sweet time. You thought you were leading her, but it was she who led you. . . . Everything on her, everything around her, rotted away. (*A pause.*)

Finally a shadow appears behind the screen. The shadow approaches.

KADIDJA: There she is!

The shadow draws closer. Then the character goes through the last screen: it is WARDA, *as adorned by* MALIKA *and* DJEMILA—*or rather as they are going to adorn her. She is holding* LEILA's *black hood in her hand. She looks surprised.*

WARDA (*laughing softly, after delicately removing the long pins set between her teeth*): Well, well!
THE MOTHER (*sharply*): What about my daughter-in-law?
KADIDJA: That's right!
WARDA: Well what do you know!
THE MOTHER: Take it easy, nitwit. You've barely passed away. You're still moving down there. And you used to be less impressionable. Where'd you see Leila? The idiot died of hunger and cold, of something or other, and she hasn't arrived yet.
WARDA (*smiling*): How would *I* know? (*She bends forward and looks down.*) Why, it's true, I haven't breathed my last yet. If only it occurs to them to finish me off. (*Showing the black hood.*) I found this on the way.
THE MOTHER: Where?

WARDA (*shrugging*): In a chest of drawers, I suppose. Underneath, inside, or behind—no Leila. (*She shakes the hood, as would a conjurer.*) Nothing.

THE MOTHER: I was present at the beginning of your death. These ladies . . .

WARDA (*interrupting her*): No. (*A pause.*) I treated myself to the death of my choice. Just as everything in my life would have been chosen if there hadn't been that stupid mess in which I found myself with my dress up, my gold petticoats unstitched, my pins twisted, my bones chipped, my collar bones out of line. . . . But my death is of my own making. I brought my art to such a pitch of perfection . . .

THE MOTHER (*smiling*): Look, idiot, look at what those ladies are doing to the pitch of perfection! (*She points to the floor where the six women are together.*)

WARDA: . . . that one evening—this evening—I went out into the darkness and the fresh air—I was so delicate and so unmeant for living out-of-doors that, as I was saying, when the fresh air struck my forehead it killed me. *That's* what happened. And I came in double-quick time and picked up this thing on the way. (*She shows the hood and tosses it away.*)

THE MOTHER (*looking upward*): No, you can say what you like, but you're not dead yet: you're in the throes.

During the scene that follows, the three women watch with great interest, and even anxiety, what is happening above, that is, on earth. The light dims, while the screen below has lit up slightly. This second screen represents the front of the brothel. It will be transparent, so that at a given moment, one can see what is taking place inside. The women who are grouped in front of the brothel are to be dressed as follows: CHIGHA, *in black;* LALLA, *in green;* AICHA, *in red;* SRIRA, *in yellow;* HABIBA, *in violet; and* AZIZA, *in orange.*

The women, who are all knitting very big black sweaters, are standing together in front of the brothel. WARDA, *who is dead, is lying stretched out on the square. But above, the dead are still present and visible, despite the dimmed light. The role of* WARDA, *below, will be played by a second actress.*

CHIGHA (*to the dead* WARDA): Your toilet waters! Your Chanel! Your red paint, pink paint, black paint! Your earrings! Your hatpins! Your style! Your underclothes, your over-clothes! Your rings! Your flowers! My man always brought a little of it back to the house and as a result you were there, in my room, and even under my bed and in my bed, on my bed, around the bed and in the closet. (*To the other women*): Let's knit. Let's knit. Without a stop. A stitch here, a stitch there. Let's knit. Let's knit.

LALLA (*to* CHIGHA): I who am to be married would never have been able to offer my belly to a man who plunged to the bottom of *this* thing. (*She pushes the corpse with her foot.*) When he came to the surface, he had a faraway look. Shellfish and mussels on his body; on his belly, a lobster, seaweed. (*Almost screaming, to* CHIGHA): What did he find there that was so terrible, tell me? Will my belly be able to give him the same look, the same shipwreck, the seaweed and the lobster?

AICHA (*to* CHIGHA *and* LALLA): When I poured my man his soup, I served a plate at an empty seat. At night, when I stretched out my hand, I found darkness. He was there but he wasn't there. And *they*, they weren't there but they *were* there. She's dead and no one'll come to condemn us. Who killed her? You? . . . You? . . . You? . . . You? . . . Me? . . . Nobody. Dead. It's a good thing we brought our knitting. We already know how to give alibis, like English ladies.

SRIRA (*to the first three*): My son never came home from the mine in a straight line. Even if he didn't enter the brothel, his

walk wove a loop around it. She was strangled by the
loops that all the men wove around her. Choked. I had
nothing to do with it. I'm knitting. (*She pushes the corpse
with her foot.*)

HABIBA (*to the four preceding women*): In short, all's well. The
brothel is again the plague spot of the town. And our
men are already what they were before the war.

AZIZA (*to all the women*): I have nothing to add, you speak so
well. But . . . some day I'd like to put my head in, just
for a second, to see how the men act with the whores.

*The six women, who were in the center of the stage, move back toward
the left, still knitting. The corpse is thus alone near the wall of the
brothel.*

CHIGHA (*to* LALLA): When are you getting married?

LALLA (*laughing*): To top it all, tomorrow!

SRIRA: Will you be able to live on what he earns?

LALLA (*sharply*): It's *I* who'll handle the money matters. If I'm
able to manage, we'll even save. I don't expect to eat like
an ogress or a princess. I can do without bracelets and
ribbons.

AZIZA: And besides, the good cuts aren't the only good ones.
Inferior ones can be good too.

SRIRA: The thing that kills me, that ruins me, isn't so much
his cigarettes, it's the habit he's got into of changing his
socks often. (*A pause.*) Does anyone have news? There's
still no word about Saïd. His stink has blended with the
stink of the town.

AICHA: Everything is changing, but very gradually.

AZIZA (*to* SRIRA): You mentioned Ommu? She's still raving.
She keeps claiming she's Kadidja on Mondays, Wednes-
days and Fridays, and Saïd's mother the other days.

AICHA: It's all her fault. I watched her in the rain, and speeches and lectures . . . in a fine rain . . .

SRIRA: Have they tried cupping?

AZIZA: Cupping. Quinine. Aspirin. Everything. No go! And when she feels better she raves louder!

MALIKA *and* DJEMILA *come out from behind the screen. They are trembling, frightened. They kneel before the dead woman and close her eyes. Then they lift her up and carry her behind the screen, where they are seen, in silhouette, laying out the corpse.*

CHIGHA (*interrupting* AZIZA): What nerve! Just look at them. They come right up to our lettuce beds to get the body.

AZIZA: What are they going to do with it?

LALLA (*laughing*): Deliver us from it.

AICHA: But then what? In any case, it was a nice idea laying out a corpse in a brothel, with whores washing and dressing it and sitting up with it. I wonder what our men are going to do? I feel like making mine go there this evening. This is one evening he ought to be there. . . .

MALIKA (*behind the screen*): They'll be there, madame! They'll all be there!

AICHA: What's she saying?

Behind the screen we see the inside of the brothel, brightly lit, contrasting with the village square, which is almost in darkness. MALIKA *and* DJEMILA, *who have placed* WARDA *on a table, are seen in silhouette. They are laying her out.*

LALLA (*laughing*): That our men are going to come and wail around the brothel tonight!

All the women laughingly mimic a funeral wail.

AICHA (*laughing very loudly*): Our men crying there? Crying or pissing? Let's not forget she's a corpse.

CHIGHA: God may strike us dead . . . (*To* LALLA): Be quiet.

LALLA: I'm too young to be afraid of God.

It is now completely dark, except in the brothel, where the two whores are seen busying themselves. They are adorning WARDA *with jewels and flowers. The village women step back farther and farther to the left, speaking very softly, and continuing to knit.*

CHIGHA: I've got to go home to put the water on to boil. And first I have to buy a box of salt and two pounds of lye. (*To* LALLA): Are you coming with me?

LALLA: No. We'd have to pass by the dump and it smells too bad.

AZIZA: Maybe the township will have it cleared. Who knows what must be rotting in it! The township's responsible.

AICHA (*to* LALLA): You were right in saying that you're young. You'll have to get used to the smell. . . .

SRIRA: In any case, it doesn't bother *me*. My man has a stronger smell. There are times I'd rather have the dump in my bed than him.

They leave the stage. Behind the screen, the two whores have finished adorning WARDA. *The hammering is heard again.*

DJEMILA: Take two or three more white roses, for her belt. And the pins.

MALIKA (*softly*): Farewell, Warda, my rose! Djemila and I are going to carry you to the cemetery . . . (*In a stern voice.*) . . . and wake up the guard, and pay him to dig a grave. Bear in mind that what happened was her own fault! I worked with her for four years. We were never able to hit it off . . . (*A pause*; *to* WARDA's *corpse*): If you hadn't provoked them . . . Have you nothing to say to us? No? Because I'm going to have to shut your mouth. (*She places several long hatpins between the corpse's teeth.*)

DJEMILA: In any case, we now have a chance: we're no longer likely to be taken back by the village. All we have to do is be ourselves. (*To* WARDA's *corpse*): You died at the height of your glory, hated by the local women. . . .

MALIKA: That'll do. Take her feet, I'll take the head. (*A pause.*) Let's get on with it.

DJEMILA: You think it's wise to go through the streets?

MALIKA: Out of the question. We might meet a customer. We'll take a short cut through the gardens. She'll get over the walls as we do. All right, let's go.

They lift the corpse and emerge from behind the screen. As they leave, they put out the light in their house. They are now before us, with the dead body, which they set on its feet. The corpse is adorned in extraordinary fashion: a large gold lace dress covered with blue roses; the shoes are made of huge pink roses. The dead woman's face is painted white. Roses and jewels on her head. Between her teeth, seven very long hatpins. When she is on her feet, DJEMILA *and* MALIKA *support her by the shoulders and walk her, very gently.*

MALIKA (*to the corpse*): Are you still with us, or are you already far away? Have you moved from the depths to the heights?

DJEMILA: Watch out for the strawberry plants and the hanging wash.

MALIKA (*out of breath*): A dead person is slow. It takes its time . . .

They leave, right.

WARDA (*above*): Their hands'll be blistered when they get back. They've gone to bury me in the dirt. (*To* THE MOTHER): In any case, if I weren't completely dead, one good shovelful in my mouth and I'd be ready for eternity.

THE SERGEANT *has returned.*

THE MOTHER: But what about Leila? . . . What about Saïd?
. . . All the same, I'm worried. . . .

KADIDJA: That's wrong of you. Put up with death and efface
yourself quietly.

WARDA: *I* started very young, with the result that I died before
my time.

THE SERGEANT (*smiling to the three women*): May I join the
cackling?

WARDA *and* KADIDJA (*smiling*): But why or why not? You're a
member of the family, pretty maiden.

THE MOTHER (*also smiling*): We knew you when you were more
sure of yourself, dealing with responsibilities.

THE SERGEANT (*still smiling*): It's because I've been dead three
days and I still don't understand a thing. . . . (*He laughs;
then, sadly.*) And I who at the noncoms' mess was always
sharp as a whip. You see how glassy-eyed I am? . . .
Well, it's because I'm shitting.

KADIDJA: Everybody—once he's dead—has to recover from the
crossing of the odd-leafed forest . . . then one drains
oneself. Of oneself.

THE SERGEANT (*smiling*): But just imagine, I died shitting . . .
squatting in the foliage, well above the hole. . . .

WARDA (*smiling*): And how is that any different from other
deceases? I too dropped my load when I came.

THE SERGEANT (*he will smile and laugh throughout the speech and
everybody will smile and laugh with him*): . . . in the foliage.
I first looked to see if there were any snakes around, you
never know, there weren't any. (*Laughter.*) In the officers'
foliage? No. A plain hole. And . . . (*He looks uneasy.*)
. . . is he still after me? (*He looks about, and the women do
likewise.*) He walked in front, actually he was always
behind me, spying on me. I can really say that I was

dogged by the Lieutenant. First, I peered into the darkness; he wasn't there. Then lowering my pants with both hands, I squatted above the hole. And it was the very moment I was squeezing (*Laughter.*) and when my eyes got glassy, the moment when, I don't know if you know it . . . let me show you (*Laughter; he squats, supported behind by* KADIDJA'*s knee and at either side, as by arm rests, by the forearms of the two other women.*) . . . when you squeeze, you get glassy-eyed, something clouds over . . . and . . . what is it that clouds over and blots out? The world? . . . The sky? . . . No. Your rank of sergeant, and that of captain! And all that goes with it: the uniform, the stripes, the decorations and the officers' school diploma when you've got one! . . . And what's left? Emptiness. I'm telling you. (*Laughter.*) I've seen officers shitting—higher officers, general officers!—their eyes: emptied. Not empty; emptied, i-e-d, emptied. The stars on their képis, no longer stars when the eyes are emptied. (*Laughter.*) Luckily, when you've stopped squeezing, when you've finished shitting, the uniform comes right back on again, the stripes, the decorations, in short, you're once again the man you were. So, with my turd half out—but still with a dopey look on my puss—I was about to stop squeezing (*Laughter.*), I was about to be the sergeant again, my vanished capital, about to understand again the beauty of martial gestures—because I was uncomfortable, not having your kindly support at the time—I was about to look at the world with eyes that know how to read service records, and . . . and? . . . and? . . . and? . . . Hey, hey? Wha . . . what's going? . . . going? . . . going? . . . going? . . . what's going? . . . going on? . . .

The screens above gradually darken while, below, DJEMILA, *who enters right, walks very quickly across the stage. Suddenly she stumbles and falls.*

THE SERGEANT: . . . my thirty-two teeth are already coming loose, but in Lyons an alley where my uncle has a mattress shop has been named after me.

This screen is now completely dark.

DJEMILA: All right, let's go . . . the cabbages and oyster plants are tripping me up! And the sheets . . . (*She pretends to be pushing aside hanging wash.*) . . . and the sheets slapping me, instead of spreading out on the ground . . . beneath my feet . . . but all the same we've got back home. . . . God, but that ground was tough digging . . . the local soil is really rich. We can be proud . . . (*She arrives at the brothel and puts on the light; and, when she gets behind the screen.*) No more Warda! The two of us'll have to handle the entire village . . .

Enter MALIKA, *right. She is followed by an Arab fighter.*

MALIKA (*in the tone of a shopkeeper*): Seven hundred francs!
NASSER (*the fighter*): Six-fifty, Malika.
MALIKA (*curtly, and showing seven fingers*): Seven hundred. (*A pause; while walking.*) Now that contempt has returned we can act demanding.
NASSER (*threateningly*): But we're warriors.
MALIKA: You now have leaders. They'll decide on the price.

SCENE SEVENTEEN

The stage is empty at first. Then it is occupied by screens arranged as follows:

Top Floor:
    I   —*White screen of the dead, at the top of the stage, left.*
    II —*White screen of the dead, at the top of the stage, center.*
    III—*White screen of the dead, at the top of the stage, right.*

Third Floor:
    IV—*Screen occupying the third floor, left, representing the prison.*
    V —*Screen representing the grocery shop, right.*

Second Floor:
    VI   —*Screen representing the brothel, left.*
    VII —*Screen representing the village square, center.*
    VIII—*Screen representing the interior of a house, right.*

    IX—*Screen occupying the entire "ground floor" of the stage.*

The pace of the following scenes, until the arrival of SAÏD, *will be very rapid. The actors themselves will set up the screens and utensils described hereafter and will draw what the screen is supposed to represent.*

The time is morning. All the actors are uncombed. They are washing themselves, yawning and stretching.

I

Top floor, high up, near the flies. First white screen of the dead, left.

KADIDJA (*speaking between yawns to someone who is probably behind the screen*): No, no . . . just for two minutes . . . two dead-man's minutes, of course . . . (*She laughs.*) Let me see it. (*She looks in the direction of the wing.*) No, the other one . . . yes . . . that one seems better, because of the velvet and the coat of arms. Can you lend it to us? I'll come and get it. . . . Put a red cushion on it. . . . No cushion?

She goes behind the screen, then, two seconds later, emerges with a very handsome gilt armchair covered with red velvet. She will place it in front of the second screen on the same level, center, near the flies, when section II begins.

II

Top floor, center. Second white screen of the dead. WARDA *has helped* THE MOTHER *carry the screen.*

WARDA (*laughing and talking to someone invisible who is in the flies*): When I get to where you are what'll you be? (*She listens.*) . . . Eh? What'll be left of you? . . . (*A pause.*) A shrug of the shoulders without the shoulders? And of me, a wiggle without my rump! (*She yawns.*)

THE MOTHER: Let them alone. Don't answer them. Other whores died before you and they weren't able to give defunct souls a hard-on. What about the village?

WARDA (*stretching and yawning*): Like fire, it's flaring up again. And, as you might imagine, thanks to us. Thanks to the brothel, it has its center. Round about is virtue. In the center is hell. Us inside. (*Bowing to* KADIDJA *and* THE MOTHER.) You outside. (KADIDJA *arrives with the armchair.*)

THE MOTHER (*looking at the armchair*): Oh! but it's too beautiful! It's too beautiful for me! . . .

KADIDJA: Try it. . . . You have to sit in comfort. And in state. It was from *your* belly that Saïd came, your ass is entitled to velvet.

THE MOTHER, *slightly intimidated, sits down.*

THE MOTHER: Like a baroness! . . . Is he going to appear?

KADIDJA (*looking down*): He's expected any moment.

THE MOTHER: But what about Leila?

WARDA: Leila. It's a sad thing to say, but I think she overshot her mark.

THE MOTHER: She had no mark.

KADIDJA: Enough about her. What about the village, what's happening to it?

WARDA: It honors you. You grow more and more beautiful as it forgets you. . . . What I mean is, it beautifies you as a result of no longer having to think of you.

THE MOTHER: What about me?

WARDA: You're the one who strangled a puking soldier in the woods. People honor you.

THE MOTHER (*crushed*): Ruined. Anyway, I've still got Saïd and Leila.

III

Top floor. The third screen of the dead, right. PIERRE, *the French soldier, is squatting and singing, while yawning.*

PIERRE (*singing*): I've known the palms, the skies, the grasses,
The artificial twats and asses,
Sold at cost at the PX
So that the boys can have some sex.

The brothel, second story, is very dimly lighted. MALIKA *is holding a burning match in one hand and seems to be guiding* HOSSEIN, *an Arab, with the other. They are silent and motionless. Then* MALIKA *quietly leads* HOSSEIN *to the door, that is, behind the screen.*

MALIKA (*in a low voice*): Watch your step! After everything I've shown you, you must think you're blind. (*She laughs softly.*)

HOSSEIN: Stop talking, whore.

MALIKA (*smiling*): In French my name means Queen. If you were polite, you'd call me Miss Queen. And you'd thank me for having made you lose your head for an hour and a half. Are you ashamed? It's because you're happy.

HOSSEIN (*threateningly*): Stop talking.

MALIKA: You're outside. So try to make yourself as liquid as possible and flow gently to your house. Good night, little trickle of urine.

She chuckles. HOSSEIN *releases* MALIKA's *hand and disappears, left.* MALIKA *goes back to the screen, but an Arab soldier (*SMAÏL*) emerges from behind it.* MALIKA *strikes a match and, with a smile, takes* SMAÏL's *hand. He disengages himself.*

MALIKA (*to* SMAÏL): Let me guide you.

SMAÏL: Don't touch me.

MALIKA (*smiling*): Because you're dressed again. You feel safe in your breeches and jacket. You're decent.

SMAÏL: Shut up!

MALIKA (*preceding him*): Come this way . . . that's right . . . careful . . . Now that you're all buttoned up again, do I disgust you?

SMAÏL: You do.

MALIKA: Then pop the buttons and zippers. No? You'd rather go away? (*He disappears, left.* MALIKA *calls after him.*) Did you pay before leaving? (*She smiles and goes back to the screen. She lights a cigarette and disappears.*)

LALLA, *wearing a yellow nightshirt, emerges from behind Screen VIII* (*second floor*), *which represents the interior of a house. She squats in front of the fireplace and lights the fire, drawing the flames. Then, she draws an empty vase on the other panel of the screen.*

A MAN'S VOICE (*from behind the screen*): And my socks?

LALLA (*brushing her hair and yawning*): In the dirty paper.

A hand passing behind the screen hangs a jacket on a nail. LALLA *goes behind the screen.* THE GROCER *and a fifteen- or sixteen-year-old boy come out from behind the screen that represents* THE GROCER'S *shop. They lean forward with curiosity; then* MALIKA *comes out from behind the brothel, looking with curiosity toward the right wing. From the prison emerges a guard who looks down—as does* THE GROCER—*at the level below.* LALLA *and her husband, who is half-dressed, come out from behind the screen that represents the interior of the house; they look in the direction of the right wing.*

THE CLERK (*to* THE GROCER): He's not rushing! It's for today, isn't it?

THE GROCER (*sternly*): Go weigh the beans. No, go count them instead.

THE CLERK: I'd like to see him.

At the same moment, coming from the left (although someone was expected at the right), appears THE CADI, *in chains, led by a policeman. He silently crosses the area which represents the village square, then disappears into the wing and immediately reappears on the third story, which he crosses, and enters the prison. All the characters disappear in turn.*

MALIKA (*before disappearing*): Oh shit, it's the Cadi!

IV

A black screen occupies the entire width of the stage on the bottom level, that is, on the floor of the stage. At the foot of this screen is a row of gilt armchairs in which the following characters were sleeping: THE SON *of Sir Harold,* SIR HAROLD, THE VAMP, THE GENERAL, THE BANKER, THE PHOTOGRAPHER, THE ACADEMICIAN, THE LEGION-NAIRE (*period of the Duke of Aumale*), THE MISSIONARY *and* MRS. BLANKENSEE. *They are in rags; their clothes are so full of holes that they are almost naked. But the rags are very decorative. They were sleeping and awaken very gently, very casually, at* SIR HAROLD'S *crowing "Cock-a-doodle-doo!"*

THE VAMP (*yawning*): You can do and say as you like, but the only true things are post cards! . . . On all the post cards from home, a church, a town hall, a river with a fisherman, a mountain. To say nothing of the hotels and restaurants. . . . (*A silence.*)

THE LEGIONNAIRE: Nobody—with a brass band in front!—has ever been able to be blasted sky-high like us . . . by a buried bomb! To scatter to every point of the horizon their right arms, heads, left legs, right feet, left feet . . .

and blood! . . . while yelling: "They shall not pass!"
(*A silence.*)

THE PHOTOGRAPHER (*yawning*): That's us. (*A silence.*)

THE BANKER: Who made Monte Carlo?

THE PHOTOGRAPHER: The post card, that's us. The art of
photography was born with us. It'll die with us. As long
as there's something at home to photograph, we'll survive.
(*A silence.*) There'll never be enough photography. (*A
silence.*)

MRS. BLANKENSEE (*to* THE BANKER): The curtains?

THE BANKER: The curtains? What about them?

MRS. BLANKENSEE: I forgot to take them. Another one of my
monumental errors. That and my late husband's pad.

THE BANKER: Even if they find it, they won't know how to use
it. They'll wear it backside front. The behind on the belly,
and the paunch on the behind.

MRS. BLANKENSEE (*shrugging*): I tell you they've understood
everything. (*A pause.*)

THE ACADEMICIAN (*anxiously*): What will they build on? I
observed them carefully throughout my stay. Their only
memories are of poverty and humiliation. . . . Yes, what
will they do? Can an art be born for the purpose of
enshrining so many facts which they themselves would
like to forget? And if there's no art, there's no culture.
Are they therefore doomed to decay? (*Several hammer
strokes are heard.*) And there they go nailing the cage. . . .
(*A silence.*)

SIR HAROLD: They've killed an innocent person!

THE BANKER: And what an idea, taking her to the desert!

SIR HAROLD: Where'd you expect them to send her?

THE ACADEMICIAN: To Poitiers. (*Professorially*). Charles Martel
is still invincible in every one of us.

SIR HAROLD: We're not going back up Spain and Gascony and
leave them this fine country. Before long the squalor that's

on them and in them will spread even to our orange trees, our olive trees.

THE MISSIONARY: It's about time you noticed it, they've just deified abjection. You'll never have the courage to conquer them.

SIR HAROLD: The army . . .

THE LEGIONNAIRE (*interrupting him roughly*): . . . never goes the limit. That's a known fact. I myself when I've been in a fury have never been able to go the limit. If I had, I'd have died. Died of pleasure. Instead of which, I've been knocked around, banged up, sold out and now have to listen to your crap. (*He spits.*) Country's rotten to the core! No leaders! Politics, no leaders! (*The hammer strokes are heard again.*)

THE VAMP: I'm the first to deplore the fact. When a general —or colonel—was given my hand to kiss, he would pass his troops in review before me. I've had, let me tell you, as many as eighteen native orderlies.

MRS. BLANKENSEE (*bitterly*): As for me, madame—or miss?— I worked. I had only one houseboy and a chambermaid and I did my own cooking. (*A silence.*)

THE MISSIONARY: What *can* be said with a certain amount of justice is that we were a pretext for their revolting. If not for us, if not—let's not be afraid to say so—for our cruelty and injustice, they'd have gone under. In all honesty, I think we're the instruments of God. Of ours and theirs.

THE BANKER: We haven't said our final word. And we at least have the possibility of entrenching ourselves behind our ancestral nobility and behind our moral nobility. We've triumphed everywhere, and long since. What do *they* have? They have nothing. (*To* THE GENERAL): Above all, don't ever allow them the opportunity of being heroes. They'd dare avail themselves of it.

THE GENERAL: That's why we attack on moonless nights. Total

invisibility. No chance of aiming at a hero's asshole.

THE MISSIONARY: They're capable of worse.

THE VAMP: Nevertheless, they did know how to look at my thighs. From a distance, of course. (*She laughs.*) Mustn't touch!

THE SERGEANT *enters among the dead.*

THE MISSIONARY: The gentle way was denied them, they demand the perilous one.

MRS. BLANKENSEE: You're making quite a to-do about a few lousy creatures. . . .

THE MISSIONARY: It's because I know—and you don't—the power of lice. . . .

MRS. BLANKENSEE: I've suffered from them, fancy that, and I cleaned myself. There are products.

THE BANKER: Yes, it's nothing to be ashamed of, my wife caught them too. Where? In the native town.

THE VAMP: The fact is that the dirtier they are the cleaner I am. They take upon themselves all the lice of the world.

THE MISSIONARY: That's what I meant.

MRS. BLANKENSEE: Well, if you did, you should have said so.

THE MISSIONARY (*reciting*): As the sea recedes, in like manner they recede from us, carrying away with them and on them, like treasures, all their wretchedness, their shame, their scabs . . . as the sea recedes, so we, receding into ourselves, recapture our glory, our legend. That which was detritus they carry away. They have run a fine comb over us.

THE BANKER (*professorially*): They polarize. (*A silence.*)

THE LEGIONNAIRE: If we had had leaders!

Hammer strokes. They all stop talking and grow drowsy again.

V

The screen represents the interior of the brothel, which we saw earlier.
MALIKA *goes to the right of the screen. She speaks to and appears to be
looking at someone who seems to be going down.*

MALIKA: Are you coming down from heaven or up from hell?
Be as light as a feather if you don't want it known that
you come to see us. . . . (MALIK, *a third Arab, appears.*)
Fork up.

MALIKA *puts out her hand, but* MALIK *runs off.* MALIKA *laughs. The
light goes on.* DJEMILA, *very scantily clad, comes out from behind the
screen. Both women will remain standing in their starched skirts and
will speak to each other in deliberate fashion. Sorry:* DJEMILA *is
holding a glass and a toothbrush. During the dialogue she will brush
her teeth.*

DJEMILA: Have all fourteen of them gone?
MALIKA: Yes, but you should've seen their naked mugs. They
use darkness as a veil. The way Leila uses her hood. For
us, the circle is thickening. . . .
DJEMILA: I don't know what, it was like before, I was in
Bordeaux, but things look all right to me. It's pretty solid
around the joint.
MALIKA: It's getting thicker and thicker. The baker's wife no
longer smiles at me when she gives me my change, and I
don't dare say anything, I'd go too far. I'd become too
beautiful.
DJEMILA: How did you girls go about things?
MALIKA: It was hardly possible to insult people, that would've
been too brutal. This isn't an age, as you can see, for
joking, so we made an effort to invent, in bed, with the
men. They must have talked about it to each other and

maybe the happiness they were given here was written on their mugs.

On the top floor, a brief dialogue is resumed.

THE MOTHER (*to* KADIDJA): I'm too excited, I don't dare look. Is there anything new?

KADIDJA: There is. Ommu has taken over from us, from you and me, and it's she who'll bring him.

THE SERGEANT, *who was resting his elbows on* THE MOTHER'*s armchair, yawns, then points to* MALIKA *and assumes a ridiculously seductive pose.*

THE SERGEANT (*laughingly*): You're right, and I admire. I too was a beautiful bitch. You and I wouldn't have been able to get along, except to give everyone a pain in the ass. . . .

MALIKA (*to* THE SERGEANT, *though looking at* DJEMILA): With me you'd have needed all the heroism you had.

THE SERGEANT (*to* MALIKA): I'm not foxy, darling, I'm . . . I'm so cunning that I'm vixenish.

MALIKA (*as above*): I'm stronger and tougher than . . .

THE SERGEANT (*as above*): I'm gentler and sweeter than . . .

MALIKA: I'm dryer and colder than . . .

THE SERGEANT (*with a great cry*): From my mouth to yours we could—however far apart—stretch threads of saliva so fine and gleaming that death . . .

WARDA (*laughing; to* THE SERGEANT): Death was under my orders. . . .

THE MOTHER *sighs. The dialogue between* MALIKA *and* DJEMILA *continues.*

DJEMILA: Continue your explanation.

MALIKA: In the past—I'm talking of before—the women weren't afraid of us. We did an honest job, but now things have changed, we make the men as happy as they'd be in hell.

DJEMILA (*attentively*): So?

MALIKA: They no longer came to us the way one goes to neighbor women, but the way one goes to a whorehouse, grazing the walls, leaving when the darkness deepens, putting on false whiskers, disguising themselves as old women, slipping under the door, going through the walls, hovering around without entering, wearing dark glasses, pretending to have made a mistake, saying that tractors and laces were sold here, sticking on a cardboard nose, stepping back to see if anyone had seen them, but, as you can imagine, what with their making themselves invisible, the brothel gleamed and sparkled.

DJEMILA (*laughing*): They polished it!

MALIKA: Like the soldier his mess tin. As for us, we returned at last to our solitude . . . and our . . . and our . . . and our truth. (*Relieved.*) It was hard. We had to invent. To discover by ourselves. At the beginning we knew nothing. But Warda, the more perverse . . .

DJEMILA: We know where that got her . . .

DJEMILA *disappears behind the screen.* MALIKA *remains upright, looking straight ahead as if without seeing.*

THE CLERK: While waiting for him to show up, do as I do, keep your thighs crossed, that'll give 'em a rest.

MALIKA (*to* THE CLERK, *contemptuously*): Give yourself a rest too, snotnose. Before long you'll have to slave if you want me to spread them. (*She spits and resumes her apparent reverie.*)

THE CLERK (*whistles*): I've been particularly attracted to

Swedish girls of late!

VI

First floor. Screen representing the interior of a house, right. LALLA *and her* HUSBAND *emerge from behind the screen.* LALLA, *her hair very neatly combed, squats in front of her* HUSBAND, *who walks about impatiently, and polishes his shoes.*

LALLA: Are you coming from work, or going?

THE HUSBAND (*looking at the vase drawn on the wall*): Coming. Couldn't you find any flowers today, a holiday? I'm coming. And you're shining my shoes because they're muddy from the workyard.

LALLA: Will things get going in a little while?

THE HUSBAND: They'll pass all bounds.

VOICE OF OMMU: It was my pair of balls . . . the little packets of arsenic I carried under my skirt to poison the well with! . . .

THE HUSBAND (*as if impatient*): The old girl! . . . She's calling Saïd! . . .

THE CLERK: The old girl needs three sticks: two canes supporting her on earth and her scream attaching her to heaven.

THE MOTHER (*admiringly*): She's going to die in anger or with a raw throat!

THE HUSBAND (*to* LALLA): Brush the tips, don't bother with the heels, I'm going out.

LALLA *stands up.*

LALLA: I want to be with you at the celebration. . . .

THE HUSBAND: We'll be there together, every man with his wife. Prepare the soup. As soon as he arrives I'll come and get you. (*Exit* THE HUSBAND *behind the screen.*)

VOICE OF OMMU: Nothing more? . . . Nothing more to save? (*A tremendous but faraway laugh.*) Must save my little heap of garbage, since that's what inspires us.

THE MOTHER: After going through the forest the old girl will get here really all naked!

When THE HUSBAND *left,* LALLA *went to the screen. Until he returns she will be drawing an enormous rose stem with very visible thorns, as described earlier by* MR. BLANKENSEE.

VII

THE CADI, *accompanied by* THE GUARD, *appears from behind the screen which represents the prison.* THE CADI *emerges as if roughly pushed.*

THE CADI (*turning around*): I swear to you . . .

THE GUARD (*appearing*): By what? A scoundrel like you couldn't have had a father or mother. . . .

THE CADI (*smiling*): Let someone lend me a mother for a minute. . . . Let some woman agree, for one minute, to be my mother and I'll swear by her!

THE GUARD (*sternly*): Get undressed. (*A pause, during which* THE CADI *starts undressing.*) I want to receive you naked. (*A pause.*) Later, I'll inspect and measure you, I'll take an inventory of your rear end. Don't worry, it's not that I want to get an eyeful, but you'll enter naked. You'll go through the door naked. (THE CADI *has just taken off his jacket.*) Where'd you get it? (*He points to the jacket.*)

THE CADI (*untying his shoes*): Stole it.

THE GUARD (*examining the jacket*): The prisoners will kid the pants off you. You've arrived too late. One now steals in battle dress and black shoes. Did you buy those socks?

THE CADI: Stole 'em.

THE GUARD (*he shrugs*): I want to receive you naked. Chuck your stuff in a corner. You'll go through the door naked. You'll be in jail. Naked, you'll be a man in jail. Then I'll toss you your stuff and you can get dressed. It won't matter any more.

THE CADI: Are there other thieves there?

THE GUARD: You don't think thieves are the only ones who are jailed? Take off your pants and get behind that. The jail's on the hill. (*He pushes him behind the screen.*) Young girls mustn't see you standing naked against the green sky.

Suddenly THE HUSBAND, *holding his bicycle, appears near the screen which represents the interior of the house. He is out of breath. He cries out to* LALLA.

THE HUSBAND: He's arriving! Come and see.

All the characters—THE CADI, THE GUARD, THE GROCER, THE CLERK, LALLA, DJEMILA, MALIKA, THE MOTHER, KADIDJA, WARDA, PIERRE—*turn around or lean forward to see who is going to arrive at the village square (center, second floor). The Europeans, below, stand up and make a half-turn in order to witness the scene. Everyone is waiting. Finally,* OMMU *arrives. The village square has filled with the cripples who were reading the posters.*

VIII

Arrival of SAÏD

First comes OMMU, *supported by two canes and by* BACHIR *and* AMER. *She is very pale: her face and hands are made up with grease paint. A kind of corpse held up by two red canes. Black shoes. Black dress.*

White hair (whitened with grease paint). She will speak in a hollow voice. She looks into the distance, squinting, in the direction of the right wing, as if following someone who is coming from afar. She makes a ninety-degree turn in the direction of the back of the stage.

OMMU: Why, he's a dwarf!

BACHIR: Because he's still far away.

OMMU: When I knew him he was big . . . and that's all that's left of him. . . . He's shrunk. (*She cries out.*) Come on, come here! . . . Straighten up, straighten up a little! . . . And get into the shade, the sun'll melt you even more . . . clever . . .

AMER: Won't you sit down?

OMMU (*curtly*): No.

THE CLERK: Are they going to fire a cannon?

OMMU (*to* SAÏD, *in the distance*): Go left . . . no . . . no, no, left . . . (*To the men around her*): He's like me, he no longer knows left from right. . . . Maybe he's turned right and I don't realize it. . . .

BACHIR (*bitingly*): We'll see to it he's set on the right path.

OMMU (*to* BACHIR): Do you know where the right path leads? . . . And animals that have no names . . . that have no colors . . . that have no shapes . . . and that are nothing. . . . (*She cries out.*) Get a move on. (*To the men who are present*): Look, he's almost as tall as we.

SALEM: You'd think he already sees himself bound hand and foot. . . . (*He laughs and the characters on all the levels—except the Europeans—laugh with him.*)

OMMU (*with her hand she makes the gesture with which one calls a chick*): Biddy . . . biddy . . . come on . . . come on . . . come along, no nonsense. Nobody wants to hurt you, they want to stuff you. . . .

HAMED: To stuff him alive? I suggest . . .

OMMU: All suggestions will be examined. We'll adopt the best.

(*To* SAÏD, *still invisible*): Approach.

LALLA (*looking in the direction of the invisible* SAÏD): He still has that gaping look, as if he were catching flies. I feel like buying him and posting him next to my pantry.

NEDJMA: With an egg like that Leila had quiet nights. Not like me.

SALEM (*laughing*): With an egg like you it was your man whose nights were quiet.

Everybody laughs.

NEDJMA: But it's you—they say—who knocked up your donkey.

Laughter.

HAMED: The donkey's going to give birth to a mule.

OMMU: Keep it up, my beauties! That's the way to receive him, the prodigal son. Give of yourselves, spare no one. (*To* SAÏD, *who is still invisible*): You needn't hurry. We have time. . . . Poor thing, on his weary dogs, no longer able to stand up straight. (*To the others*): Make way for him. Push aside. Push aside the houses and gardens too. (*She moves a screen, and when it has been moved, we see behind it the cage that some workmen are completing.*) And the whole town if necessary to receive the native son in state! Push aside the night . . . push back the wheels of the planets to the edge of the wheel of heaven . .. and let them fall into the void to clear the way for us! Come on . . . Come along . . . three more steps . . . two more . . . one . . . there . . . (*Enter* SAÏD.) Bow. (SAÏD *bows, removing his hat.*) Well?

SAÏD: Well, here I am again. . . . I wasn't so far away. (*Everyone bursts out laughing.*) Were you expecting me?

BACHIR: We wanted to give you a welcoming party. It's being prepared. Here and among the dead. (*Gravely.*)

You've been very useful to us.

SAÏD (*with nobility*): I imagine so. But it's been quite an effort and I'd like to rest a bit.

NEDJMA (*laughing*): And what if you were going to swing at the end of a rope?

SAÏD: I wouldn't mind: between heaven and earth . . .

OMMU: We'll see later what's to be done with you, but we were supposed to receive you and pay our respects. You need homage. And I, aspirin. My aspirin! (BACHIR *hands her two tablets which she swallows.*) You were circling round the village for quite a while. . . .

SAÏD: I got lost.

OMMU: The more you lost your way in the stones and in the woods, the deeper you sank into another region to which it wasn't easy for us to descend. Though we made every effort: anger, grief, insults, fever—I have a hundred and seven point two!—delirium . . . as you see me now, I'm wandering, I'm rambling, through the woods! (*She laughs.*) In showing us the way, you and your admirable spouse taught us how one must lose oneself. . . . (*She laughs again.*)

SAÏD: In order to judge me . . .

AMER (*laughing*): There are no more judges, there are only thieves, murderers, fire-brands. . . .

OMMU: Don't tremble like that, we're not going to hurt you. As regards betrayal, you did what you could, and there we're obliged to say that you didn't achieve much. (*Everybody laughs.*) I know, I know, the intention was good. That's why we'll take it into account. But it's become impossible to judge you. If no one has gone as far as you . . .

NASSER (*as if outraged, and bombastically*): When the hunter's out with his gun, he less often sees feathers—of seagull or albatross—snowing in the sky than I when I sent her flying and falling and snowing in her veils and skirts and wings. . . .

OMMU (*to* NASSER): Who, the little girl in her communion dress, the little dear? You shot and killed her in a rage. With Saïd it's another matter. He was alone. And Saïd, if we were able to sustain our frenzy to the bitter end, or almost, heedless of the gazes that were judging us, it was because we had the luck to have you—not as a model, no, not as a model!—to have you, the couple you made with Leila. . . . By the way, about Leila?

SAÏD: Leila?

OMMU (*anxiously*): Did you love her?

SAÏD (*laughing*): How could I have been able to? . . .

THE MOTHER (*from above; relieved*): Fortunately. And I saw to it.

SAÏD (*continuing*): . . . she did everything to put a damper on me. As for me . . . I'm not saying I was never on the point of weakening, a tenderness, like the shadow of a leaf trembling above us, ready to alight, but I'd take hold of myself. No, no, as far as that goes, you needn't worry. She died raging. And as for me, if I croak . . .

OMMU (*continuing*): Not as a model, no. As a flag. (*A silence.*)

THE ACADEMICIAN (*with disgust*): I told you so. They were bound to come around to it, to emblems and banners. But what they've chosen does not do them honor.

THE VAMP: *We* have too *many* heroes. And too much glory and gold on our cloth.

THE LEGIONNAIRE: *You* say that? (*Disgustedly.*) There're no more leaders!

THE MISSIONARY: They're organizing. That's the beginning of a ceremonial that's going to bind them together more firmly than anything else. (*He sniffs the air.*) I recognize a familiar smell. . . .

MALIKA: Even I—I whom they call Satin Skin when the candle's blown out . . .

CHIGHA: But Turkish Towel when the wick is lit. (*Everyone laughs.*)

MALIKA: Satin Skin that I was, I had goose flesh when he went up the stairs. (*Everyone laughs. A combatant pulls her behind the screen that represents the brothel.*)

OMMU: The knowledge that his holy family was sinking into muck gave us all goose flesh. . . . And even now, whatever skin and bone I still have has goose flesh. . . . The lords of yesterday will tell the lords of today that nothing must be protected so much as a little heap of garbage. . . . Let no one ever throw out all her sweepings . . .

LALLA: I always put a pinch of it under the radio.

CHIGHA: And I, in the vest pockets . . .

AZIZA: And I in the salt cellar to salt the broth . . .

OMMU (*as if in a state of hallucination*): And if ever some day . . . (*To* SAÏD): Don't move! . . . the forest's getting darker and darker, and it's hot . . . it's because I've got to go by a pond and the water in it isn't water. . . . And if ever some day the sun falls on our world in a golden rain—one never knows—keep a little mudpile in reserve in a corner. . . . Should the sun reflect and its rays, which give me such a pain in my head, in my poor head riddled with arrows . . .

THE HUSBAND: An hour that's lost can be made up, but a half day is lost for good. So let's get on with the festivities! (*He takes a swig from his bottle.*)

CHIGHA (*to* SAÏD): It seems that when one's within fifty feet of the main sewer one can tell from the odor that Leila's bobbing up and down there. . . . If she's the one who's being transformed into whiffs of stink, we're not likely to lose our memory.

OMMU: Once I'm dead you'll need all the reminders you can get. I don't think I'm capable, with my rot alone, both here and in heaven, to prevent you from longing for sweetness and light. . . . The wind's going to carry me off . . . I feel it passing through my bones the way it passes through a flute. . . . I've almost no more weight, a quarter of an ounce in all . . . you'll have to rely on yourselves. . . . As for Saïd, we're going to use him. . . .

SAÏD: Isn't it all over?

OMMU: We're embalming your sordidness, your shittiness.

SAÏD: Does that mean I'm going to keep rotting until the end of the world in order to rot the world, is that what it means?

OMMU: Means or doesn't mean means nothing. We were looking for you, Saïd, looking for you, it took my fever and second sight to ferret you out. You're here, and we're holding on to you, you eel, slipperier than a girl. We've got to—come on, quick!—we've got to embalm your shittiness, so that none of it's lost. The end, my end, is approaching, I'm approaching the end, we're meeting head-on, midway, and who'll take over when I'm gone? . . . (*She seems oppressed.*) You see it's urgent. . . .

BACHIR (*approaching*): An aspirin, old girl?

OMMU: No. I need fever in order to gibber away, just as fever needs me if it wants to do the same. Kadidja told you more about it than I will. . . .

SALEM: She was dead when she did.

OMMU: . . . and the forest isn't eternal, I realize it. If Kadidja was dead when she told it, I've got to croak in order to tell it, for my madness is already departing . . . the festivities driving on . . . lightning operation in a driving rain! The ceremony in the twinkling of an eye . . . Saïd, Saïd! . . . larger than life! . . . Your brow in the nebulae and your feet on the ocean . . .

THE CLERK: Got to eat spinach!

LALLA (*arranging her hair*): Where do we find a trough for him to eat from?

The next four speeches—those of SAÏD, THE GUARD, BACHIR *and* OMMU—*are to be spoken with bursts of laughter.*

SAÏD: My brow in the nebulae! And my feet? . . .

THE GUARD (*as if to himself*): And standing till the end of time.

BACHIR: His voice a hundred thousand trumpets; his smell all the clouds in the universe.

OMMU (*to* SAÏD): . . . You're going to surpass your own height.

CHIGHA: We'll organize to knit him socks to his new size!

SAÏD: I'll do what you ask, but . . .

OMMU (*feverishly*): Don't worry about anything. We'll do everything ourselves. . . . We know the technique . . . it'll all go off smoothly. . . .

SAÏD (*with sudden violence*): You're going to kill me first, aren't you? Then do it right away! You were waiting for me, it's my party. . . .

OMMU (*more and more feverishly*): Don't irritate me. My head's on fire and, in the fire of the bells, my eyes in my own head, the wind in my thigh bone, ice under my petticoat, it's dead that we want you, dead, but it's alive not dead. . . .

SAÏD (*furiously*): That's leaving me dead alive!

OMMU (*threateningly*): It's neither dead nor alive! . . . All honor to sordidness! Storm the living! . . . Legion of Honor, a comma on the whitewash of latrines!

SAÏD (*still furious*): That's leaving me dead alive!

OMMU (*almost in a trance*): And if it were necessary to sing, to sing . . . If it were necessary to invent Saïd . . . If it were necessary word by word, here and there, to spit, to slobber a whole story . . . written or recited . . . to slobber the Saïd story . . .

THE GUARD (*laughing and exclaiming*): I've spent nights . . . I'll sing his nights of love with Leila . . . I've spent nights, days, listening to men under sentence of death. They all sing, but not all of them aloud. . . .

OMMU: To croak! . . . With the belly open and the story oozing out . . . The dogs . . .

THE GUARD (*continuing his preceding speech*): . . . aloud. With some it's only a vibration of the strings of the calf. A breath of air passes over them. A song arises. Over that harp . . .

SAÏD (*furiously*): That's not me, Saïd! On neither the wind of the harps nor the quivering of a calf.

OMMU: . . . the dogs will say we're of the race of dogs ... . It's a story for them to carry from door to door, at night . . .

THE GUARD (*laughing*): A song arises! I learned to sing like them, from the calf, from the bend of the knee, and even from the gut! (*No one laughs.*) What, you're laughing? (*Severely.*) Haven't you ever heard the guts of the condemned sing? It's because you don't listen. (*He announces, with stateliness.*) The romance of Saïd and Leila, by the gut of a condemned man. (*A long silence.*)

OMMU (*laughing, feverishly*): And carried, add, carried at night from door to door by the severed heads of dogs, related by the neck-stumps of dogs. . . .

THE COMBATANT (*who has just come out from behind the screen of the brothel and is buttoning himself*): Fine. That's a pretty speech, old gal. You can let yourself talk that way, you're dead. I was listening while giving Malika a workout. (*To the men*): Boys, I recommend tearing off a piece during the unveiling of a monument to the war dead, while listening to the patriotic speech! . . . (*To* OMMU): But we're alive, I'm speaking of those of us still alive, so tell me if the severed heads of the mutts are supposed to bring us, us up there, the story of Saïd?

THE CADI (*as if to himself, but forcefully*): The fools!

OMMU (*to* THE COMBATANT): We have nothing to do with you. You reason.

THE COMBATANT: If you want to organize, you've got to reason.

What are we combatants entitled to?

A silence. OMMU *seems to be reflecting. Finally she speaks.*

OMMU: To shut up and go die in the sun. (*Very clearly and plainly.*) For some time now, ever since we've been wearing ourselves out here with wearing out our miseries of all kinds, you, up there, have been organizing your death in high and harmonious fashion.

THE COMBATANT: For the efficacy of combat.

OMMU (*like an automaton*): For the esthetics of decease.

THE MOTHER: She's made it! She's out of the forest. She's coming our way.

OMMU (*as above*): Soldier! . . . Soldier of ours, young prickhead, there are truths that must never be applied, those that must be made to live through the song they've become. Go die facing the enemy. Your death is no truer than my raving. You and your pals are proof that we need a Saïd. . . .

THE COMBATANT: What you say may be true for you and me, but what about the others? (*He snickers.*) When the fighting is over and they're back home?

A rather long silence. A SECOND COMBATANT *comes out of the brothel and joins the first.*

OMMU: Don't let him think he's squelched *me*! You needed an emblem that rises up from the dead, that denies life. (*Mournfully.*) ". . . When the fighting is over and they're back home . . ." As if that meant a damn to me! Certain truths are not applicable, otherwise they'd die. . . . They mustn't die but must live through the song they've become. . . . Long live the song.

THE COMBATANT: Neither I nor my friends fought so that it

would sing in you, Caroline. We did fight, if you like, for the love of fighting, for pomp and circumstance and the new order . . . .

OMMU: Go lie down, take a little rest after that solemn thought. Anyway, we didn't go and get killed . . .

THE COMBATANT (*ironically*): Then who went and killed you?

A THIRD COMBATANT *leaves the brothel and, by the same stairway, joins the first two.*

OMMU: I'm killing myself repeating it to you! Didn't go and get killed to protect pacha, caïd, grocer, grease-ball barber, surveyor—to hell with them, but to preserve, preciously, our Saïd . . . and his saintly wife . . .

All the dead start laughing and applauding.

THE COMBATANT (*to the dead*): That'll do. You're not going to appropriate the victory or determine the meaning it's to be given. That's for us the living to decide. (*The men on the village square applaud.*) Good.

A fourth combatant, like the third, comes out of the brothel, then a fifth.

THE COMBATANT (*looking about him*): I'm safe on that side. I feel that logic arms men's minds. Before long we'll all be reasoners. . . . (*To* SAÏD): As for you, we forgive you. You'll come with us and change your skin. And even your mug.

OMMU (*she laughs*): Oh! How nice! . . . Forgive, how nice! . . . Forgive rose and veil of the Virgin! . . . Forgive lighted taper, altar cloth, lace and hands on our brows . . .

THE SECOND COMBATANT: Forgive or not, enough sordidness, shittiness . . .

OMMU: You march in step . . .

THE THIRD COMBATANT: When the corporal orders "March," we fall into step.

OMMU: We're keeping Saïd. In order to protect his squalidness . . . and we're also going to water his squalidness so that it grows.

THE COMBATANT (*to* SAÏD): Come here to me. (SAÏD *hesitates.*) I'm not asking you to become a soldier. . . . (*The dead burst into laughter; among them we see* THE MOTHER, KADIDJA, THE SERGEANT, PIERRE, THE GENERAL, WARDA, MR. BLANKENSEE *and* THE LIEUTENANT.) Shut up! Lie down, you dead! You've had your funerals, your honors and your splendors, whatever stinking meat's entitled to. Very well. (*The dead laugh softly.*) Allow us to live peacefully. (*To* SAÏD): I told you to come here.

OMMU (*holding* SAÏD *back*): And I, to stay there.

SAÏD (*gently, and after looking about the square*): To the old gal, to the soldiers, to all of you, I say shit.

He steps away from the group and is about to leave, but the five combatants take out their revolvers and aim at him.

THE COMBATANT: Halt!

SAÏD *stops and turns around.*

OMMU (*rushing in front of* THE COMBATANT): You're not going to bump him off? You're not going to steal him from us? You're not going . . . why, you're nuts, you're batty . . . you're not going to destroy our treasure. . . . It's through him that we breathe. . . . (*She has a fit of coughing and bends double.*) Might as well croak right away. . . .

THE SECOND COMBATANT (*pointing to* SAÏD): We're not going to
let him keep on . . .

THE CLERK: Suspense!

THE THIRD COMBATANT (*to* SAÏD): All right, come. We'll wipe
the slate clean and start all over.

SAÏD *seems to hesitate.*

OMMU (*with a cry*): Escape! Clear out of yourself! Through your
mouth or asshole, but clear out, don't stay here!

THE COMBATANT (*to* SAÏD, *with an air of severity*): And *I* tell
you . . .

SAÏD (*gently*): I'm very much in demand. I can set my price. . . .

*A long murmur among the dead, who look at each other and seem to be
taking counsel mutely. Suddenly,* THE MOTHER *explodes.*

THE MOTHER (*screaming*): Saïd! . . . (*Everyone looks at her.*) Saïd!
. . . you're not going to give in? She-dog that I am,
she-dog big with a mongrel pup, I kept you in my guts
not to become one more one less! A dog's life, kicks in
the ribs and maybe rabies! Less than a patch of nettles,
less than what you're worth, until noon today—it's noon
sharp—I thought it was hatred that was leading *me*,
Saïd! . . . Let me speak to you in a whisper . . . (*All the
others, except the Europeans, cover their heads with the flaps of
their jackets or dresses. The dead turn away, cover their ears, shut
their eyes.*) . . . in a whisper, child. Listen . . . (SAÏD, *looking
at the audience, that is, turning his back to his* MOTHER, *cups his
hand over his ear. He is all attention.*) Here's what I'm saying
in your ear: me, the belly you came out of, kicked out by
the living and the dead, a soldier was entangled and I
idiotically got wound up in the straps, and it's he I finally
gave birth to. He's at my side. And on account of that

lousy break the town council is thinking of naming the
village square after me. It's shattered me, Saïd . . .
you . . .

SAÏD (*in a rather low voice*): That's laying it on thick. They
haven't found your body . . .

THE MOTHER: According to hearsay, I've been buried in a
pauper's grave with the others who were tortured. Saïd,
beware. I'm counting on you . . .

SAÏD (*in a somewhat anxious voice*): Leila . . . Leila's succeeded . . .

THE MOTHER: I'm not the mother of Leila.

SAÏD: You brought her to perfection.

THE MOTHER: I brought *you* into the *world*. Make a getaway.
Don't let yourself be conned by either the old girl or the
soldiers. Don't serve either of them, don't serve any
purpose whatever. I think they're going to make up a
song about you. The words have been written. People are
humming it. It's in the air. (*She screams.*) Saïd, squelch
the inspiration, shit on them! . . .

SAÏD: They've already taken quite a load from me. If I add
any more . . .

A muttering among the dead.

THE SERGEANT (*turning around: to* SAÏD): You're on the right
track, Saïd, do as I do! All the lousy things I did made
me luminous. I shone, Saïd!

THE VAMP: Bravo, Sergeant! You did some pretty raw ones.
(*She laughs.*) From tearing off toenails to . . .

THE ACADEMICIAN: You're out of your mind! The plaque with
his name on it in the alley is being unveiled this morning.
Nobody knows what he did except that he died.

MRS. BLANKENSEE: That's not so. I was told . . . (*She falls asleep
again.*)

THE BANKER: Gossip.

THE ACADEMICIAN (*very sadly*): One can't build on what he did. It's no longer done. *They* can, but not we (*Professorially.*) So, the Sergeant has his plaque, because nothing is known; there's the difference.

OMMU, *whose face is still hidden by her skirt, approaches softly. Suddenly, she uncovers.*

OMMU (*to* SAÏD, *on the Q.T.*): Now's your chance to make a getaway. Clear out while they're arguing!

SAÏD *hesitates and makes a gesture as if to leave.*

THE COMBATANT (*turning about brusquely*): Stay there! (SAÏD *hesitates again, then leaves.*) Fire!

The five revolvers of the combatants fire five shots. Everyone looks behind the screen, where SAÏD *has gone. A body is heard collapsing. Everybody, except the dead and* OMMU, *turns around with a look of consternation.*

MRS. BLANKENSEE (*awakening with a start*): Always those noises beneath my window. (*She goes back to sleep.*)
OMMU: I won't find time today again to kick off. Burying this one, screaming at that one· I'll live to a hundred. (*To* BACHIR): An aspirin.

BACHIR *hands her an aspirin, which she swallows. Everyone has withdrawn, except two combatants and* OMMU. *Below,* THE BANKER. THE LEGIONNAIRE, THE VAMP, *etc., who had stood up when* SAÏD *arrived, sit down again to doze.*

THE COMBATANT (*to* OMMU): Don't be upset, old gal. You'll be six feet under before long.

OMMU (*shrugging*): First Saïd has to be tossed into the dump.

She leaves, right, supported by her two canes and by BACHIR *and* AMER. *The two combatants follow her. All the other actors, except the dead, remove the screens and objects which they brought in at the beginning of the scene. A long silence. All the dead, above, watch the living clear the stage. They remain alone.*

KADIDJA (*victoriously*): They're moving out! They're moving out! . . .

THE SERGEANT: There it is! . . . I've got my plaque! (*He laughs.*) I sure got it, the plaque at the corner of the alley where my uncle's a mattress maker. Got it! People resented my handsome mug, but my beauty served as a setting for my cruelty—that jewel!

The Europeans wake up and leave.

THE MOTHER (*anxiously*): What about Saïd? Is he coming?

THE SERGEANT: My beauty grew with my cruelty, one heightening the other. And the rays of their love, when I took off my pants, gilded my behind! (*He laughs.*)

THE MOTHER: Saïd! . . . I'll simply have to wait for him. . . .

KADIDJA (*laughing*): Don't bother. He'll no more be back than will Leila.

THE MOTHER: Then where is he? In a song?

KADIDJA *extends her palms with a gesture expressive of doubt.*

During the last two or three speeches, the dead carried off their screens. THE MOTHER *leaves last, with her armchair. The stage is empty. It's all over.*